INCOMPARABLE
EXPLORATIONS IN THE CHARACTER OF GOD

ANDREW WILSON

David C Cook®
transforming lives together

For Rachel
You bring me praise at the city gates!

INCOMPARABLE
Published by David C. Cook
4050 Lee Vance View
Colorado Springs, CO 80918 U.S.A.

David C. Cook Distribution Canada
55 Woodslee Avenue, Paris, Ontario, Canada N3L 3E5

David C. Cook U.K., Kingsway Communications
Eastbourne, East Sussex BN23 6NT, England

David C. Cook and the graphic circle C logo
are registered trademarks of Cook Communications Ministries.

The Web site addresses recommended throughout this book are offered as a resource to you. These Web sites are not intended in any way to be or imply an endorsement on the part of David C. Cook, nor do we vouch for their content.

LCCN 2008929267
ISBN 978-1-4347-6756-1

© 2007 Andrew Wilson
First edition of *Incomparable* published by Survivor, an imprint of Kingsway Communications,
© 2007 Andrew Wilson, ISBN 978-184291-281-2; cover design by Mark Prentice

The Team: Richard Herkes, Melanie Larson, Amy Kiechlin, Jack Campbell, and Susan Vannaman
Second Edition Cover Design: Amy Kiechlin
Interior Design: Alexis Goodman, The Visual Republic

Printed in the United States of America
Second Edition 2008

1 2 3 4 5 6 7 8 9 10
052008

CONTENTS

EXPLORATION II: The Names of God

EXPLORATION III: God in Three Persons

Acknowledgments

Hillary Clinton once said that it took a village to raise a child. I don't know whether I agree, but it certainly takes a village to write a book. More people than could possibly be mentioned have contributed ideas, support, and encouragement, most of them from Kings Church Eastbourne, and for the twelve months I have been working on this project, I have been truly amazed by how far people have gone to help.

The most remarkable example has been Karen Solway's hospitality. Despite never having met either Rachel or me, she let us live with her in Maryland for three months while this book was being written. I could never have completed it without the space and time I had in the States, and writing each day in Washington DC's book shops and coffee shops only increased my belief that the world needs to know "I AM" more than anything else. Thank you, Karen.

The other indispensable blessing I received was being released by Kings Church to write the book in the first place. Graham Marsh and Dave Dean, the elders, have been hugely supportive of the project throughout, and allowing me two months in which I did nothing but write and answer e-mails was proof, if it were needed, of the church's commitment to being a center for teaching and resourcing. I am humbled by their kindness, their trust, and their (often very amusing) input.

I could say the same for everyone at Kings who has contributed to the actual content. It honestly is the case that, when you're writing, every person who even shows interest in what you're doing is gold dust, so there could be hundreds of people on this list. But I received a combination of good advice, great ideas and inspiring encouragement from Andy Johnston, Oli and Wendy Stevens, Phil James (who cowrote one of the reflections), Paul Johnson, Andy Thorpe, Sally Blundell, Martin Cooper, Les Moir, and

Jez Field. The prayer support from my Life Group was much appreciated, Richard and Jenny James were extremely generous to us at exactly the right time, and Eric and Rose Pavey let me have their house in France for a few days—they may even recognize the description. It is a privilege to be at such a church.

Beyond Kings a number of others have significantly shaped what follows. My parents introduced me to the God this book is about, and it was a thorough introduction whose influence can be found on almost every page: First they got me into the Bible, then Judson Cornwall, A. W. Tozer, John Piper, David Pawson, and J. I. Packer, and they bought me my first Tom Wright books as well. Every Impact student I have had has asked questions, made points, and argued interpretations, without which this book would be much more abstract and much less interesting. John Hosier, Joel Virgo, John Groves, Reuben Lyons, Stef Liston, and all of the AWE team have been hugely encouraging, saying small things that have made big differences. Phil Moore's friendship, example, and commentary on the Pentateuch have been invaluable. And of course any twenty-seven-year-old who wants to write a book about God needs great editors; Richard Herkes has commissioned, shaped, fiddled with, and improved everything I have written, and Mel Larson took on the challenge of translating an unashamedly English book into something that both sides of the Atlantic could understand (apparently "rugby tackling a snooker table" would have been particularly mystifying). I am very grateful to all of them.

The most influential person of all, though, has been Rachel. Not just because she is incredibly beautiful, always encouraging, and ever inspiring, but because she genuinely had more ideas and insights than anyone else. If you come across anything of practical relevance or unusual passion, it is probably hers. Truly, the Lord has provided!

FOREWORD

A wonderful move of recent years has brought worship leaders and songwriters together with theologians and thinkers. Why is this so important? Well, as Andrew Wilson says, theology matters because it fuels worship.

We have the responsibility and the joy to allow God to continue to shape, reshape, and fuel our worship. In Romans 12:11, we read, "Never be lacking in zeal, but keep your spiritual fervor, serving the Lord." We constantly need fresh revelation and understanding of who God is. The hymn writer John Newton spoke for so many of us when he wrote,

> Weak is the effort of my heart and cold my warmest thought.
> But when I see thee as thou art, I'll praise thee as I ought.

In each chapter of Andrew Wilson's wonderful book, we catch a greater glimpse of our Most High God. We are left amazed, stunned, humbled, convicted, exhilarated, excited, refreshed, and inspired.

Often our worship dries up because we fail to passionately explore the fullness of who God is. We dumb him down to an earthly level, failing to see that he is above and beyond our human understanding. It is important to remember that God is not made in our image. On the contrary, we are made in his. "For I am God and not man—the Holy One among you" (Hos. 11:9).

Wayne Grudem captured this concept beautifully when he wrote,

> The difference between God's being and ours is more than the
> difference between the sun and a candle, more than the differ-
> ence between the ocean and a raindrop, more than the difference
> between the arctic ice cap and a snow flake, more than the

difference between the universe and the room we are sitting in: God's being is qualitatively different. No limitation or imperfection in creation should be projected on to our thought of God. He is the creator; all else is creaturely. All else can pass away in an instant; he necessarily exists forever.[1]

When we encounter God—uncreated, all-powerful, self-existent, maker of all things, uncontained, unbreakable, unfathomable, and infinite—we find perspective. We learn to embrace the smallness of who we are and marvel in the vastness of who he is. Earthly pleasures can no longer take the place of knowing God and being known by him. We are left ruined. Satisfied and dissatisfied at the same time. We begin on a journey, thirsting for more of God, desperate to understand more clearly the character and nature of God. When we encounter the reality of God, true worship is the outcome.

The church needs to recapture a big picture of all that God is. Our view and understanding of him will have a significant impact on our worship. As Graham Kendrick said, "Worship is a response and will grow or shrink in direct proportion to our view of Him." So, let us continually dig a bit deeper and press on into the mystery and character of God. This book is an amazing place to start. I pray that not only will Andrew's words inform and stretch your mind; but that they will also inspire your heart to worship and open your mouth to praise.

—Tim Hughes
Singer, songwriter, and worship leader

Endnote

1. *Wayne Grudem,* Bible Doctrine *(Downers Grove, IL: InterVarsity, 1999), 72.*

INTRODUCTION

• • • • • •

This book is about God. Quite unashamedly. The reflections are short, and hopefully the illustrations make it relatively easy to understand, but the subject matter is the most difficult, exciting, meaty, and wonderful topic there is: the living God.

If that sounds like a dangerous challenge, it probably is. But I believe that there is nothing anywhere that is more worth reading about and responding to than the character of God. In fact, I am convinced that if your knowledge of God doesn't grow, then neither will you. Let me give you a few reasons why I think theology, the study of God, matters.

Theology matters because of Panida. Panida was fourteen when she was taken from her home in Thailand to Malaysia by a sex trafficker. She arrived in a city she had never seen before, and was told that she had been sold. She was told she had to have sex with between five and ten clients each night, every night, if she was to pay off the debt.

If she refused, she would be beaten, and would not be allowed to eat. She was allowed to sleep between five a.m. and three p.m., in a locked and barred room with seven other slave girls, and was forbidden from even putting her head out of the window. Helpless and terrified, she sat on her bed, waiting.

Thousands of miles away, a group of lawyers and investigators had seen something of the character of God. They had read Amos, and the Psalms, and Isaiah, and encountered the God who championed the cause of orphans and widows and victims. Taking seriously God's anger at injustice and the biblical commandments to set free the oppressed, they set up an organization that (among other things) prosecuted child traffickers and freed sex slaves, funded entirely by the charitable donations of others who had also gained revelation about the God of justice. International Justice Mission (IJM) was born.

Panida never saw her first client. The night she was going to start, a raid was conducted with local police, based on an undercover investigation done by IJM. She was set free without ever having to pay or prostitute herself, and ninety-four other girls were released in the same series of raids—ninety-four rape victims made in the image of God, who were set free because some lawyers they had never met read their Bibles and discovered something about the character of the living God.[1] Theology matters.

Theology matters because of Dave. A tall, sociable salesman in a small town in England, Dave had no background in Christianity and no interest in getting one. Like millions around him, he was destined for an eternity without God. That is, until his first child was born. Looking down at the miracle of life in his hands, Dave couldn't believe it was an accident, and marveled at the wisdom that God, if he existed, must have in order to create his daughter. It was a life-changing moment. He and his wife Julie repented of their sins, got baptized, and committed themselves to their local church. Twenty years later, having brought up two Christian children, given generously to further the gospel, and run a marriage course numerous times, Dave and Julie are moving three thousand miles away to help build the church in Canada. Revelation of the wisdom of the creator God changed a man, a family, and a church.

There are millions of Daves around the world. Sadly, there remain some Panidas, and there is still work to be done. But it is theology, the revelation of who God is, that saves Daves and frees slaves. Being convinced of God's sovereignty is the only thing that can strengthen a martyr or inspire someone to plant a church in the Muslim world. Seeing his holiness is the only thing that can produce the kinds of revival we read about in church history. Understanding his Fatherhood is the only thing that can mend people broken by abuse and fear. Grasping his grace is the only way to get free of legalism, false expectations, perfectionism, and who knows how many other modern sicknesses. Seeing how scary God is serves as the ultimate weapon against sin. You and I were transformed by revelation of who God is—what Paul calls "the light of the knowledge of the glory of God in the face of Jesus Christ" (2 Cor. 4:6). But that was not the end of our need for theology. It was the start.

Theology also matters for the church as a whole. It can often seem like the world is taunting us, whether through liberal theologians, newspaper columnists, scriptwriters, or whoever, like the Rabshakeh in Isaiah 36:4,

"On what do you rest this trust of yours?" The answer, of course, is the same as it was for Hezekiah: on Yahweh of hosts. Knowing the God in whom we place our trust is the only secure foundation we have.

The character of God is the only basis we have for establishing churches in the first place. Knowing the God of Israel is our foundation for community on earth, and the ultimate answer to those who would prefer to opt out of local church altogether. The multicolored wisdom of God is our foundation for building multiracial, multigenerational, and socially diverse congregations in a world where people like spending time among their own. It is also the reason to establish indigenous churches in countries where very few locals have been converted. If the church is not based on the character of God, it is just a club that people can feel free to join on their own terms. But if it is, community is not optional, because we are expressing who God is to the world.

Theology matters because of mission. In Scripture, the missionary task is always rooted in the character of God. Psalmists cry out for the nations to praise him, and apostles give up their lives to reach new people groups, because of his excellent attributes: "Let the nations be glad, for you judge the peoples with equity!" "That the Gentiles might glorify God for his mercy." "To the praise of the glory of his grace." And so on. When people stop caring about who God is, the imperative for mission fizzles out.

So does the basis for mission's success. This swings both ways: People can believe God is so independent of us that he doesn't need us (like the infamous leader who told William Carey that God could save the heathens "without your help"), or they cannot believe he is truly sovereign, so there is no point in praying. For the apostles, though,

God's sovereign freedom was the basis of their missionary success: "And as many as were appointed to eternal life believed" (Acts 13:48). His all-surpassing goodness and glorious grace meant that any sacrifice, any persecution or torture, even death itself, was worth it. Good theology will always result in a sacrificial, zealous, joyful mission.

Good theology will also stop the church from becoming irrelevant on social issues. Every year, secular Western liberals write volumes to argue that Jesus was a misunderstood teacher of tolerance, cryptic wisdom, and love for fellow men, who would have had no problem with anything like sexual immorality or abortion or divorce—which all makes him sound suspiciously like a secular Western liberal. On the other hand, rich conservatives can produce an equally distorted mirror image, in which God has lots to say about the family, liberty, and individual responsibility, but nothing at all to say about greed, social justice, or care for the poor—which all makes him sound suspiciously like a rich conservative. Knowing the God of the Bible will protect us from such mistakes. The more we know the God of justice and the God of holiness, the more the global church may end up fighting child slavery in Asia, domestic violence in Africa, materialism in North America, and sexual immorality in Europe with the same vigor.

All of these things—freeing sex slaves, saving individual men and women, transforming people's thinking, establishing churches, going to unreached people groups with the gospel, engaging with social issues around the world—are important. To my mind, they are all but one of the most important things we ever do. But the most important thing we do, and the biggest reason that theology is important, is worship: glorifying God himself.

Theology fuels worship. We cannot worship what we do not know; we cannot delight in what we have not seen. When I compliment my wife, Rachel, I ground what I say in facts about her. If I didn't know her very well, my relationship with her, and the honor I could give her, would be very limited. It is the same with God. We praise him because we know him. The world's best worshippers are theologians—not necessarily professional scholars, or academics, but theologians, people who know the character of God because they have read about him, gotten to know him, and experienced him in their lives. Missionaries like William Carey, James Hudson Taylor, and Jim Elliot. Songwriters like Charles Wesley, Augustus Toplady, and Isaac Watts, and for that matter Stuart Townend, Darlene Zschech, and Matt Redman. Preachers like George White-field, Charles Spurgeon, and Jonathan Edwards. These people are worshippers because they are theologians. They have said and done great things because they know God.

Knowing the character of God is like putting heavy logs in the fireplace: When the fire of worship is lit, it burns hotter, brighter, and longer than the guy's down the road who used paper. But that metaphor has a flip side—there is no use in theology that does not turn into worship. Logs that just sit there on the hearth would have been better off staying in the forest. When we learn about objects, it enhances our brains and equips us to use them; when we learn about people, it enhances our relationships and equips us to serve them; when we learn about God, it enhances our lives and equips us to worship him. So if our theology does not regularly and joyfully lead us to worship, then something is wrong.

For this reason, all of the reflections in this book are written with worship in mind. Some reflections are followed by a brief *Selah*, designed to give some practical application from what we have been studying; others are left deliberately open-ended. Some reflections are quite complex; others are extremely simple. But my prayer is that all of them, no matter what their content, help you delight in the King of Kings. I would like to think that people could use these reflections in any setting—in their devotional times, to prepare preaching, to read on the train, or even in the downstairs bathroom. Theology and worship are for all times and all places. But however you use them, I hope they will provoke you to praise the I AM that they are trying to describe.

"For from him and through him and to him are all things. To him be glory forever. Amen" (Rom. 11:36).

Endnote
1. For more information, see International Justice Mission's Web site, www.ijm.org.

......

EXPLORATION I
The Being of God

......

GOD EXISTS

• • • • • •

The fool says in his heart, "There is no God."
—Psalm 14:1

The Bible never tries to prove the existence of God. It would be like a math textbook proving that 1 + 1 = 2, or a historian trying to show that there was such a thing as the past—there would be no point. To the Bible writers, God's existence is foundational, essential, and startlingly obvious. So anyone who does not believe in God, the psalmist says, is quite simply a fool. Lots of clever people since then have come up with ways of proving God's existence, and some of these can be useful. But it is interesting that—in a book spanning two thousand years of history and with stories about all sorts of people who don't believe in him—the Bible never presents an argument for God's existence. It is so obvious, it doesn't need to be argued for.

Many people today think the opposite. Lots of people believe that nonbelief in God is the default view, and science has removed the need to add God into the picture. People take it for granted that God doesn't exist, and if you say he does, they will want you to prove it scientifically. If you ask them to prove scientifically what they believe, of course, they are very unlikely to be able to—but mostly, they will not see this as a problem, because it seems that the majority agree with them.

There are two problems with this. One, the majority is often dangerously wrong. The majority of German officers in the 1930s agreed with persecuting Jews; the majority of nineteenth-century Europeans thought black people were second-class citizens; the majority of medieval scientists thought the world was flat. But also, lots of beliefs we hold—often, the most important ones!—are just not provable scientifically.

Take the statement: "For something to be true, it must be provable scientifically." Can that statement be proved scientifically? Can you do an experiment in a lab to demonstrate that it is true? Or how about, "My daughter loves me"? How can that very important statement ever be proven? The fact is, we believe things because they make sense of the world as we see it, not because some outside authority (like scientific proof) says they are true. So the real question is: How does belief or nonbelief in God make sense of the world around us?

You see, every view of the world has to provide an explanation for every fact there is. People who do not believe in God still have to account for beauty, the fact that the world came into being in the first place, the occurrence of miracles, the awareness in people that there is such a thing as evil, the existence of things like conscience and

emotions, and the sense of God that seems to be present in every civilization we have ever discovered. Often the explanations provided for
these facts are so ridiculous that they call into question the worldview
itself (like the ways atheists try to explain Jesus' empty tomb). Denying the existence of God creates many more problems than it solves.

The biblical perspective, on the other hand, accounts for the
unbelief of other people in terms of sin. Look at Paul's argument in
Romans 1:18–20:

> For the wrath of God is revealed from heaven against
> all ungodliness and unrighteousness of men, who by
> their unrighteousness suppress the truth. For what can
> be known about God is plain to them, because God has
> shown it to them. For his invisible attributes, namely, his
> eternal power and divine nature, have been clearly per-
> ceived, ever since the creation of the world, in the things
> that have been made. So they are without excuse.

People don't believe in God because they suppress the truth. They
want to be independent of God, without accountability for their actions,
and so they don't want there to be a God. As Thomas Nagel, professor
of philosophy and law at New York University, wrote recently, "It isn't
just that I don't believe in God and, naturally, hope that I'm right in
my belief. It's that I hope that there is no God! I don't want there to be
a God; I don't want the universe to be like that."[1]

It is simply foolishness and sin that lead people to deny that God
exists. The Bible never argues for God's existence, but titles it as the

foundation stone of all thinking and living, because God's character is so clearly evident in creation. From morality to mercy, from miracles to mountains, God's existence is displayed in all things. Only the fool denies it.

Endnote
1. Thomas Nagel, The Last Word *(New York: OUP, 1997), 130.*

God the Beginning

· · · · · ·

In the beginning, God …
—Genesis 1:1

In the beginning, God. What a way to start! No lengthy explanations or arguments, just a simple few words that show God was always there. Questions like "Who made God?" or "What was there before him?" are shown here to be as irrelevant as they are silly. God is, was, and always will be the beginning of all things.

As with God's existence, there are many people today who argue that God was not the beginning, because we can't prove he was. We have already seen how poor this argument is. On the other hand, it is important that we understand that our belief in God's pre-existence— the idea that he was there before anything else came to be—is not logically ridiculous, but actually the most likely explanation of why things are as they are.

John Piper gives a helpful way of thinking about this.[1] Go back in time in your mind to the beginning of time, before the Big Bang, before anything we can scientifically understand had happened. We don't know what started it all—it could have been a gas, or it could have been a person. It's a 50/50 shot. We will never be able to turn up a fossil and find out which it was. The only way of coming to a conclusion about it is to look at the world around us, and see whether the person explanation or the gas explanation looks more likely. Does the universe carry the characteristics of a person who created it? Or is it all a random collection of atoms, which in some cases have formed living things?

To some scientists, the universe is exactly that: a random series of matter and events that show no sign of a personal God. Richard Dawkins, the famous scientist and atheist, said this: "In a universe of blind physical forces and genetic replication, some people are going to get hurt, other people are going to get lucky, and you won't find a rhyme or reason in it, nor any justice. The universe we observe has precisely the properties we should expect if there is, at bottom, no design, no purpose, no evil, and no good, nothing but blind pitiless indifference ... DNA neither knows nor cares. DNA just is. And we dance to its music."[2]

To most people (including many scientists!), this is ridiculous.[3] Quite apart from the social and moral dangers of believing that all people, from Mother Teresa to Hitler, are simply dancing to the music of their DNA, there are a number of properties in the universe that suggest design, purpose, evil, and good. The fact that we are aware of "good" or "evil'" at all is an obvious example. If everything in the world is "blind pitiless indifference," why do we have a sense of good or bad? Why aren't we all striving to have as many offspring as possible, as you would expect if there were no personal qualities in the universe? Conscience is another example. In evolutionary terms it is difficult to explain, whereas if we are created by a person, it makes perfect sense. Or take our attitude to things like time and death—two of the most certain and normal things there are. Why do we fear death, and mourn for people, sometimes people we don't even know? Why do all cultures known to us observe burial rituals of some kind? Why are we surprised by death, and surprised even by the passing of time? C. S. Lewis, in fact, sees this as strong evidence for man's eternal destiny, arguing that it is "as though the universal form of our experience were again and again a novelty. It is as strange as if a fish were repeatedly surprised at the wetness of water. And that would be strange indeed; unless of course the fish were destined, one day, to become a land animal."[4]

I am inclined to agree. That God was there in the beginning, not a gas or an atom or an explosion, is indicated by the host of our universe's design features that point to a person.

The Bible does not go into this, of course. As with the existence of God, his pre-existence is just assumed. Yet it is also present throughout Scripture, from the first verse of Genesis to the first verse of John's gospel to the final chapter of the whole Bible (see Rev. 22:13). In the beginning, God. It's as simple as that.

Endnotes
1. John Piper, Desiring God: Meditations of a Christian Hedonist *(Sisters, OR: Multnomah, 2003), 322f.*
2. *Richard Dawkins,* River Out of Eden: A Darwinian View of Life *(New York: Basic*

Books, 1995), 133. For a fuller response to Dawkins, see Andrew Wilson, Deluded by Dawkins? *(Eastbourne, UK: Kingsway, 2007).*

3. *For a convincing argument for this position, see the various works of Alister McGrath, including* Dawkins' God: Genes, Memes and the Meaning of Life *(Oxford: Blackwell, 2004), and* The Dawkins Delusion *(Downers Grove, IL: InterVarsity, 2007; London: SPCK, 2007).*

4. *C. S. Lewis,* Reflections on the Psalms *(New York: Harcourt, 1958), 138.*

GOD THE CREATOR

• • • • • •

Worthy are you, our Lord and God, to receive glory and honor and power,
for you created all things, and by your will they existed and were created.
—Revelation 4:11

God created all things. This is one of the most important teachings
in the Bible, because it establishes the relationship between God and
everything else. If God created all things, then lots of very common
beliefs about the universe are simply wrong. Think about it: Materialism
(the idea that the material, physical world is all there is) must be wrong,
because there is a God. Dualism (both God and everything else have
always existed side by side) must be wrong, because God created matter.
Pantheism (God is in everything) and panentheism (everything is part
of God) must both be wrong, because God is distinct from what he has
created. God created all things, and by his will they exist.

But if creation is one of the Bible's most important teachings, it is also one of its most contested, and confidence in it needs to be restored. We cannot go into the ins and outs of the debate here, but evolution is widely believed to make the Bible's account of creation impossible, and, although this is not true, it still holds a lot of influence at the popular level.[1] It is worth pointing out, though, that people may choose evolution over creation, not because the science points that way (in many areas it doesn't), but because it is a theory that does not need God. As a leading Harvard biologist admits:

> We take the side of science in spite of the patent absurdity of some of its constructs ... because we have a prior commitment, a commitment to materialism. It is not that the methods and institutions of science somehow compel us to accept a material explanation of the phenomenal world, but, on the contrary, that we are forced by our *a priori* [fundamental] adherence to material causes to create an apparatus of investigation and a set of concepts that produce material explanations, no matter how counterintuitive, no matter how mystifying to the uninitiated. Moreover, that materialism is absolute, for we cannot allow a Divine Foot in the door.[2]

So beware of anyone who thinks they are the only one without presuppositions. It usually means theirs are so dominant that they don't even notice them any longer!

The widespread use of the word "nature," even among Christians, also suggests that confidence in the biblical view of creation needs to be restored. The Bible never talks about "nature," but about "creatures," because creatures point to a creator, whereas nature just is. It is important to recognize this: God should be given honor and glory for his creation, rather than everything being credited to some impersonal force like nature. This is the point of the verse quoted above—because God created all things, because things only exist in and through him, he is worthy to receive glory and honor and power. Remember, the origin of sin is in knowing God is there without giving him thanks or glory as we ought to (Rom. 1:21).

In Genesis 1, God is said to "create" three things: the heavens and the earth (1:1), living creatures (1:21), and man in his image (1:27). Of everything else it is said "he made." It is as if the word "create" is reserved for those moments when God makes something completely unprecedented, something that has never been done before, a new sort of something (matter, living creatures, and man as the image of God). Whether or not this is the case, the Bible makes it clear that everything that exists came about because God created it; God did not shape something that already was, but brought into being something that had never been, simply by the power of his word. That's why Genesis 1 keeps repeating the phrase, "And God said."

In fact, Genesis 1 seems to be doing more than just accounting for how things came into being. It is making a powerful statement about the true God as opposed to the false gods other nations believed in at the time. Other people believed in gods who fought and struggled with one another; the God of Genesis created simply by the power of his word. Other cultures worshipped the sun, moon, and stars; the God of Genesis created them, and indeed created things (including light itself) before them. Other nations saw great sea monsters as symbols of chaos; the God of Genesis created these as well, and "saw that it was good." In short, the God of Genesis is in a totally different category from everything else that exists.

The fact that God is the creator should make us stand in awe. Nicky Gumbel writes:

> On 20th August 1977, Voyager II, the inter-planetary probe launched to observe and transmit to earth data about the outer planetary system, set off from earth traveling faster than the speed of a bullet (90,000 miles per hour). On 28th August 1989, it reached planet Neptune, 2,700 million miles from the earth. Voyager II then left the solar system. It will not come within one light year of any star for 958,000 years. In our galaxy there are 100,000 million stars, like our sun. Our galaxy is one of 100,000 million galaxies. In a throwaway line in Genesis, the writer tells us, "He also made the stars" (Genesis 1:16). Such is his power.[3]

God created all things. If he had done nothing else, this alone would make him worthy of glory and honor and power.

Endnotes
1. A good, readable, recent contribution to the debate from a Christian point of view is given in Lee Strobel's The Case for a Creator *(Grand Rapids, MI: Zondervan, 2004).*
2. Richard Lewontin, "Billions and Billions of Demons," The New York Review *(January 9, 1997), 31.*
3. Nicky Gumbel, Questions of Life *(Eastbourne, UK: Kingsway, 1995), 89.*

READ AND REFLECT

Psalm 104 is a powerful way of focusing our minds on the astonishing range of God's creation. As you read through the psalm, notice the way in which it mirrors the structure of Genesis 1: light and space, sea and sky, plants and trees, sun and moon, sea creatures, earth creatures, and finally rest and rejoicing.

It may help you worship if you read it out loud in praise to God. If you learn the words, you can pray or sing them next time you go for a walk.

Bless Yahweh, O my soul! O Yahweh my God, you are very great! You are clothed with splendor and majesty, covering yourself with light as with a garment, stretching out the heavens like a tent. He lays the beams of his chambers on the waters; he makes the clouds his chariot; he rides on the wings of the wind; he makes his messengers winds, his ministers a flaming fire.

He set the earth on its foundations, so that it should never be moved. You covered it with the deep as with a garment; the

*waters stood above the mountains. At your rebuke they fled; at
the sound of your thunder they took to flight. The mountains
rose, the valleys sank down to the place that you appointed for
them. You set a boundary that they may not pass, so that they
might not again cover the earth. You make springs gush forth
in the valleys; they flow between the hills; they give drink to
every beast of the field; the wild donkeys quench their thirst.
Beside them the birds of the heavens dwell; they sing among the
branches. From your lofty abode you water the mountains; the
earth is satisfied with the fruit of your work.*

*You cause the grass to grow for the livestock and plants
for man to cultivate, that he may bring forth food from
the earth and wine to gladden the heart of man, oil to
make his face shine and bread to strengthen man's heart.
The trees of Yahweh are watered abundantly, the cedars
of Lebanon that he planted. In them the birds build their
nests; the stork has her home in the fir trees. The high
mountains are for the wild goats; the rocks are a refuge for
the rock badgers.*

*He made the moon to mark the seasons; the sun knows its
time for setting. You make darkness, and it is night, when all
the beasts of the forest creep about. The young lions roar for
their prey, seeking their food from God. When the sun rises,
they steal away and lie down in their dens. Man goes out to
his work and to his labor until the evening.*

O Yahweh, how manifold are your works! In wisdom have you made them all; the earth is full of your creatures. Here is the sea, great and wide, which teems with creatures innumerable, living things both small and great. There go the ships, and Leviathan, which you formed to play in it.

These all look to you, to give them their food in due season. When you give it to them, they gather it up; when you open your hand, they are filled with good things. When you hide your face, they are dismayed; when you take away their breath, they die and return to their dust. When you send forth your Spirit, they are created, and you renew the face of the ground.

May the glory of Yahweh endure forever; may Yahweh rejoice in his works, who looks on the earth and it trembles, who touches the mountains and they smoke! I will sing to Yahweh as long as I live; I will sing praise to my God while I have being. May my meditation be pleasing to him, for I rejoice in Yahweh. Let sinners be consumed from the earth, and let the wicked be no more! Bless Yahweh, O my soul! Praise Yahweh!

GOD THE CRAFTSMAN

· · · · · ·

Where were you when I laid the foundation of the earth? Tell me,
if you have understanding. Who determined its measurements—
surely you know! Or who stretched the line upon it? On what
were its bases sunk, or who laid its cornerstone, when the morn-
ing stars sang together and all the sons of God shouted for joy?
—Job 38:4–7

Not only did God create all things, but he also crafted them. He built them, brought shape to them, designed them. God didn't haphazardly scatter things about and hope for the best; he made everything with care, and the wonder of creation bears this out. God is a master craftsman.

Consider the passage from Job. Job and his friends have been questioning and speculating about God's character and justice for thirty-five chapters, until God finally speaks to them "out of the whirlwind" (if this ever happens to you, you may be in trouble!). The string of rhetorical questions that follow are designed to show Job the absolute care with which God has made all things, as well as the absolute power he wields to do what he pleases. God pictures himself variously as a ground worker (laying foundations for the earth); an architect (determining its measurements and stretching the line upon it); a builder (sinking its bases); and a bricklayer (laying its cornerstone). In other words, God is responsible for every part of creation, and nothing has been made without his design and execution.

If we think about this at the biggest level, it inspires reverence and fear. The stars, unthinkably large balls of gas and fire that appear as small dots in our sky because they are so far away, were designed, crafted, and built by the God we worship. If we go in the other direction, we can reflect in astonishment at the work ethic of ants (as in Proverbs 6:6–8), or the astounding beauty of tropical fish, or the speed of a peregrine falcon, or the variety of creatures hidden in the depths of the sea or in mountain hideouts that humankind has not even discovered yet. And we can see the design and craftsmanship of God in each of them.

God's skill has a further implication, though, one which should affect the way we see ourselves. God the craftsman paid special attention to designing and building one creature in particular, one which he described as being made "in the image of God" (Gen. 1:27)—the human being. If God was so careful in his craftsmanship while making the earth, imagine what it was like with humans! Perhaps it was this revelation that led David to sing: "You formed my inward parts; you knitted me together in my mother's womb. I praise you, for I am fearfully and wonderfully made. Wonderful are your works; my soul knows it very well. My frame was not hidden from you, when I was being made in secret, intricately woven in the depths of the earth" (Ps. 139:13–15).

God did not make one mistake in his creation. Nothing got made because God was having a bad day, or could not be bothered, not even the smallest creatures. Take diatoms, for instance. There are over a hundred thousand known species of these invisibly tiny algae-like creatures. There are up to a million of them in one teaspoonful of lake water, and some estimates suggest they supply 35 percent of the world's oxygen. Every one of them testifies to the craftsmanship of God.

If God carefully designed every diatom, how much more can we be sure that he made us, his people, carefully and wonderfully! Your heart, for instance, pumps enough blood during your lifetime to fill a string of tanker trucks stretching from Boston to Washington DC, and it pumps it 186 million miles. An even more astonishing example of God's craftsmanship is the human brain, perhaps the most baffling and amazing created thing on earth:

> The human brain is heralded for its staggering complexity and processing capacity. Its hundred billion neurons and several-hundred-trillion synaptic connections can process and exchange large amounts of information over a distributed network of brain tissue in a matter of milliseconds. Such massive parallel-processing capacity permits our brains to analyze complex images in one-tenth of a second, allowing us to visually experience the richness of

the world. Likewise, the storage capacity of the human brain is nearly infinite. During our life-time, our brain will have amassed 109 to 1020 bits of information, which is more than fifty-thousand times the amount of text contained in the U.S. Library of Congress, or more than five times the amount of the total printed material in the world![1]

God not only creates all things, he crafts them. He designs every string of DNA—each containing as much information as the Encyclopedia Britannica—and fashions together every neuron, breathes his life into every creature, lays the foundations for every landform, and constructs every galaxy. And as the pinnacle of his creativity, the Mona Lisa in his collection, God made you and me in his image.

What a privilege, and what a responsibility. But also, what an amazing witness to the craftsmanship and skill of our creator God.

Endnote
1. *René Marois, "Capacity Limits of Information Processing in the Brain,"* Phi Kappa Phi Forum, *Winter 2005.*

God Sustains

. . . . . .

Lift up your eyes on high and see: who created these? He who brings
out their host by number, calling them all by name, by the greatness
of his might, and because he is strong in power not one is missing.
—Isaiah 40:26

If God stopped sustaining the universe, it would collapse. We don't
very often think about this, but it's true, and quite scary. We are happy
with a picture of God making the world and then leaving it—the
absentee landlord theory, which we call deism, and which is very common today—but the idea of our existence being dependent on God
on an ongoing basis is frightening. Yet this is exactly what Isaiah is
saying in this passage. If anything in the universe could sustain itself,
it would surely be the stars, the largest of all created things. Yet God
not only created them, but he also brings them out by their number,
knowing each of them by name. In other words, he sustains them.

I love that phrase "because he is strong in power not one is missing." Imagine for a moment God stopped sustaining the stars by the strength of his power. Now imagine the headlines: ALPHA CENTAURI DISAPPEARANCE SHOCK. MILKY WAY MISSING, SAY EXPERTS. God's power is needed for every last one of the billions of stars to continue existing, and if he decided to stop, they would vanish. So, for that matter, could we.

The thing is, we can often picture God's relationship with creation as being static: He made it, so it is here now and always will be. The Bible, though, sees creation as being dynamic: The universe only continues to exist because God keeps sustaining it. If I make a model, or a cupboard, or a computer, I do not need to keep sustaining their existence, because once I have built them, they stay there unless something destroys them— they have an existence that is independent of their maker. But if I make a sound, like singing a note, the sound stops as soon as I stop making it. The sound, in fact, only exists because of its relationship with me, and has no existence of its own. The universe is like that. If God stopped sustaining it, it would have no basis to continue being there.

This is hugely important. It means we do not only rely on God for something that happened in the past (creation), but something that he continues to do in the present and—because he has promised— into the future (sustaining). This is as true for our heartbeats as it is for the heavens, as true for the grass as it is for the galaxies, because nothing can exist without God's continued power. As Elihu puts it in Job 34:14–15: "If he should set his heart to it and gather to himself his spirit and his breath, all flesh would perish together, and man would return to dust."

All breath, all life, belongs to God, and it is his to give out as he pleases. Our default setting, if you like, is that we expire. It is only through God's continued intervention, his ongoing sustaining power, that we survive.

It is therefore no exaggeration when it says in Hebrews 1:3 that Jesus—fully God as he is—"upholds the universe by the word of his power." What a statement! The great Puritan John Owen comments on this verse:

> Such is the nature and condition of the universe, that it could not subsist a moment, nor could anything in it act regularly unto its appointed end, without the continued supportment, guidance, influence, disposal, of the Son of God … And this abundantly discovers the vanity and folly of those who make use of the creation in an opposition unto the Lord Jesus Christ and His peculiar interest in the world. His own power is the very ground on which they stand in their opposition unto Him; and all things which they use against Him consist in Him; their very lives are at the disposal of Him whom they oppose.[1]

Consider it: Even those who oppose Jesus are themselves being sustained by his powerful word. When Judas betrayed him, when Caiaphas insulted him, when the soldiers crucified him, each of them was only existing because of the "word of his power."

The fact that God sustains all things, even the stars, should cause us both to fear and to worship. To fear, because we have a God we are dependent upon if we are even to continue breathing. To worship, because we have a God who is active in the world at all times, and therefore will never be removed from our situation. Next time there is a clear night sky, look up and remember: God created all these, calling them by name, bringing them out by number. And because he is strong in power, not one is missing.

Endnote
1. *John Owen,* Epistle to the Hebrews *(Grand Rapids MI: Kregel, 1968 [1668–74]), 6.*

God Is Incomparable

· · · · · ·

To whom then will you liken God, or what likeness compare with him?
—Isaiah 40:18

Have you ever noticed how hard it is to describe God? If someone was to come up to you and ask you to explain what God is like, you would probably end up listing things that are true about him—that he is good, powerful, holy, and so on—but without really describing him all that well. Teachings like the Trinity, and Jesus being both fully man and fully God, are impossible to explain properly. Even little children can ask you questions about God that you cannot answer. And this can be quite infuriating, especially if you are the sort of person who likes knowing everything. God is truly indescribable.

The reason for this is simple: We describe things by comparing them. We explain unknown things by referring to known things. If you were to ask me what turkey tasted like, I might say it was like chicken, only darker and richer. If you had never eaten chicken, I would say it was like duck, only less fatty. If you had never tasted poultry before, I might compare it to another meat, like lamb, only much lighter and softer. Somehow, I would find a way of explaining turkey in terms of things you had previously come across. That is the way we explain things.

This becomes more difficult when things are a long way from our experience. If you read science books at school trying to explain distances in space, or the size of galaxies, or how small an electron is, the odds are that you found it pretty difficult to grasp. This is because those things are so big or so small that you don't have anything obvious to compare them with. The best you can do is use an illustration to try and help you understand (for instance: If the earth is the size of a pea, the sun is about eighty yards away, and the nearest star is on the opposite side of the world). Space is so big that it is hard to find things to compare with it.

God is like this but much, much more so. He cannot be compared to anything or anyone. In fact, comparing God to something always ends up limiting him. Yes, he is larger than the mountains, but he is *so much* larger that the comparison is pretty meaningless. Yes, Jesus shines brighter than the sun, but he is *so much* brighter that the picture doesn't get us much closer to understanding him. Nothing in creation can be compared to God without it making God seem far smaller than he is.

That is why the images used in the Bible to describe God are so varied—from the animal kingdom alone, we have lion and lamb and eagle and man and leopard and bear and ox and dove—because one of these, taken alone, would emphasize some of God's characteristics and ignore many others. The same is true of anything else we might compare him to. Saying that a great sportsman or musician is "incomparable" is not really true, because we could always say he or she is "like so-and-so, only better." Comparing God to anyone or anything, though, is impossible, because the comparison falls so far short.

This is what Isaiah is saying here. In a world where virtually every tribe had their own god, it was tempting for some Israelites to think of the true God as just one of these—their God, perhaps, but one who could be compared to the gods of other nations. Isaiah will have none of this. Who, he asks, can you possibly compare God to? An idol? They are made by man, totally unable to move; in what sense can they be compared to the creator of all things? He continues in 40:21–23: "Do you not know? Do you not hear? Has it not been told you from the beginning? Have you not understood from the foundations of the earth? It is he who sits above the circle of the earth, and its inhabitants are like grasshoppers; who stretches out the heavens like a curtain, and spreads them like a tent to dwell in; who brings princes to nothing, and makes the rulers of the earth as emptiness."

God cannot be compared to other gods, to earthly rulers, to the sky above, or to anything in creation. He is simply in a completely different league. Comparisons and (much more so) physical images of God are totally inadequate and limit our understanding of God. However much we may want to explain God in nice, neat ways, God transcends our categories. He is, quite literally, incomparable.

God Is Unknowable, Yet Knowable

• • • • • •

No one knows the Son except the Father, and no one knows the Father
except the Son and anyone to whom the Son chooses to reveal him.
—*Matthew 11:27*

The Bible is full of puzzling ideas. Scripture makes it clear that we
cannot compare God to anything or anyone else, that he is beyond
our knowledge, that we cannot fit him into our categories. At the same
time, though, it clearly teaches that we can know him, and that we
should in fact spend our lives "increasing in the knowledge of God"
(Col. 1:10). So we cannot know him, yet we can know him? It all
sounds very confusing. But actually, if you think about it, this is the
case with all personal knowledge.

When we are dealing with facts, it is possible to know something
completely. I know that 5 + 5 = 10, and I know everything about that
statement. When we are dealing with people, on the other hand, it is

very different. I know my wife, Rachel, better than anyone else in fact, but there are numerous things about her I don't know. I don't always know what she's thinking, I don't understand all her feelings, there are numerous experiences she has had that I have not shared, and so on. So I know her, but I don't know her fully. This is because people are far more complex than mathematical equations.

God, of course, is far more complex than people, so it is impossible to know him fully. But that does not mean that we cannot know him at all, because we can know all sorts of things about him. Imagine if I said to myself, "I will never know Rachel fully, because I will never be able to share all her experiences and think her thoughts. So I am not going to bother getting to know her better." It would be ridiculous, wouldn't it? Instead, what I do is to spend my life learning more about her, although I know I will never know her completely. It is the same with God.

Or take space. Space is incomprehensibly, unknowably, breathtakingly vast, like God. But, as with God, some people know almost nothing about space, and others spend their lives looking through telescopes into its mysteries, even though they will never understand it fully. In fact, as with God, often the people who know most about space are the ones who realize how much there is still to discover. Understanding God (like understanding space) includes realizing you can't understand him! As the great theologian Herman Bavinck wrote, "God's incomprehensibility does not deny his knowability, it requires it and affirms it. The unsearchable riches of the Divine Being form a necessary and important part of our knowledge of God."[1]

The amazing thing about knowing God, though, is that it doesn't come just by studying or investigation, but by revelation. Look at what Jesus says in the verse above: "No one knows the Father except the Son and anyone to whom the Son chooses to reveal him." In other words, we cannot know God unless he is revealed to us. If God did not reveal himself, we might be able to guess that there was a god of sorts, but we would be hopelessly misguided as to what he was like. If you want evidence for this, read some of the stories of the Greek gods! When there is no revelation, man makes gods in his own image, gods who fight and squabble and fornicate. We need revelation to have any hope of knowing God.

The fact that we only know God by revelation does not mean, of course, that studying his character is unimportant. You presumably agree, otherwise you wouldn't be reading this! But you sometimes hear people say, "I don't want to know *about* God, I just want to know *him*." This is silly. Imagine trying to know someone really well without ever finding out anything about them—their likes and dislikes, their personality, their history, their hopes and dreams. Knowing about someone is part of knowing them, and it is the same with God. Yet we must always remember that our knowledge of God does not come from us, but from him. Be very careful if you hear yourself saying, "I like to think of God as …" or "To me, God is …" Our knowledge of God completely depends on his revelation to us.

But praise God—he has revealed himself! Jesus, we are told here, chooses to reveal the Father to people, and that is how we know him. There is no learning or wisdom in all the world that is capable of fathoming or understanding God, but God takes the initiative and reveals himself to us in ways we can relate to: by living within us through his Holy Spirit, by inspiring a book, and (most astonishingly) by becoming a man. So God is unknowable, in that we can never fully understand him and cannot know him without revelation, but he is knowable, because he has revealed himself through Jesus. No one knows the Father except the Son, and those to whom the Son chooses to reveal him.

Endnote
1. *Herman Bavinck,* Gereformeerde Dogmatiek *Volume II (Kampen: J. H. Bos, 1897), 25 (author's translation).*

 # PAUSE AND PRAY

In the first few centuries of the church, great thinkers and godly saints wrestled with the question of how to communicate what they knew about God. What they came up with were a series of creeds, still used in many churches around the world today, which highlight the main things we can know about God (while by no means covering everything!). The following is perhaps the greatest of these: the Nicene Creed, originally written in 325 and then revised into this form in 381. For over sixteen centuries, Christians of all varieties have been using this as a way of describing what they know about God.

Whether or not you come from an established church tradition, you might find it helpful to pray through it, thanking God for each truth as you go.

> *I believe in one God, the Father Almighty, Maker of heaven and earth, and of all things visible and invisible.*

> *And in one Lord Jesus Christ, the only-begotten Son of God, begotten of the Father before all worlds; God of God, Light of Light, very God of very God; begotten, not made,*

being of one substance with the Father, by whom all things were made. Who, for us men and for our salvation, came down from heaven, and was incarnate by the Holy Spirit of the virgin Mary, and was made man; and was crucified also for us under Pontius Pilate. He suffered and was buried; and the third day He rose again, according to the Scriptures; and ascended into heaven, and sits on the right hand of the Father; and He shall come again, with glory, to judge the living and the dead; whose kingdom shall have no end.

And I believe in the Holy Spirit, the Lord and Giver of Life; who proceeds from the Father and the Son; who with the Father and the Son together is worshipped and glorified; who spoke by the prophets.

And I believe one holy catholic and apostolic Church. I acknowledge one baptism for the remission of sins; and I look for the resurrection of the dead, and the life of the world to come. Amen.

God Is Good

● ● ● ● ● ●

O, taste and see that Yahweh is good! Blessed is
the man who takes refuge in him!
—Psalm 34:8

Some ideas are so simple that we miss them. Lots of books get written
about God's sovereignty and our choices, or about the Trinity, but
there are far fewer books about his goodness. In fact, I don't think I've
ever heard a sermon on God being good. When the Psalms, as they so
often do, say "Yahweh is good," we unconsciously ignore it. Yes, God
is good, but we know that. Move on to the next verse.

But what does it actually mean for the psalmist to say that God is
good? We might think it is obvious, but it could mean one of at least
three things. It could be a property of him. It could be an opinion
about him. Or it could be a definition of him. In fact, in the context of
Psalm 34, it is probably all three.

In one sense, to say "God is good" is to give one of his properties. If I say "milk is white," I am describing what milk is like by telling you something that happens to be true about it. It doesn't define it—milk is white, but then so are window frames and teeth and fridges—but it tells you that it is white as opposed to brown or pink or blue, and so if you see something colored, it might be a lot of things, but it isn't pure milk. Saying God is good, in one sense, is like this. David is giving a description of God, so we know that (among other things) he is good, which means he does good things and doesn't do bad things or mediocre things or things that don't quite work out. Therefore, if we see something less than good, it might be a lot of things, but it isn't God.

Now imagine, instead of saying "milk is white," I said, "milk is a whitish liquid containing proteins, fats, lactose, and various vitamins and minerals produced by the mammary glands of all mature female mammals after they have given birth."[1] Suddenly my statement has gotten bigger. This is not a description anymore, but a definition: Anywhere you find this type of substance, you will, by definition, have milk, and vice versa. In the same way, God is good by definition; anywhere you find goodness you will, by definition, have God, and vice versa. You can't have God without goodness, and you can't have goodness without God. This is the teaching of the whole of Scripture:

"And God saw everything that he had made, and behold, it was very good" (Gen. 1:31).

"No one is good except God alone" (Mark 10:18).

"And we know that for those who love God all things work together for good" (Rom. 8:28).

"Those who seek Yahweh lack no good thing" (Ps. 34:10).

And so on.

But what if I say "milk is nice"? I have now moved from saying something objective to something subjective; it is an opinion, based on something I have found through experience to be true. In fact, it is something you can test only by trying it yourself. This is the clearest meaning of the cry, "Oh, taste and see that Yahweh is good!" The psalmist has got a list of examples of God's goodness to him—like deliverance (v. 4), provision (v. 10), being heard (v. 15), and so on—and he is urging us as readers to experience this goodness ourselves. Knowing God is good but never experiencing his goodness is as useless as knowing the definition of milk and never drinking it.

However, we need to clarify something here. Some people misunderstand the idea that Yahweh is good and take it to mean that bad things will never happen. Then, because the results of the Fall—things like death and sin and sickness and abuse and earthquakes—still happen, they get angry with God. But this is not the psalmist's understanding of God's goodness. In verse 19, he makes the remarkable announcement, "Many are the afflictions of the righteous," which is the exact opposite of what many people today would think. Even with a good God, who is sovereign over everything and has the power to do whatever he likes, good people still suffer. The punch line comes in the next phrase, though: "But Yahweh delivers him out of them all." Evil happens, but "none of those who take refuge in him will be condemned" (34:22).

It could not be any other way. God is shown to be good from our experience, and can be described as (among other things) very good, but he is also good by definition. He has never been faced with a catch-22 situation, forced to choose between the lesser of two evils, or flummoxed into a decision that was anything less than completely good. Therefore if God has done something, it is good, end of story. We may well not understand why God has done it, of course. Job didn't either. But we can be confident, based on Scripture and on our experience, that as sure as milk is white, Yahweh is good. Taste and see!

Endnote
1. The American Heritage Dictionary of the English Language, *Fourth Edition.*

GOD IS SPIRIT

· · · · · ·

God is spirit, and those who worship him must
worship in spirit and in truth.
—John 4:24

We tend to struggle with things we cannot see. Child psychologists say that if you show young babies a toy and then remove it from their line of sight, they do not realize that the toy still exists. But to be honest, adults can live a bit like this too. That's why we live our daily lives as if famine in Somalia or child prostitution in Cambodia are not real (and why charities try to remind us that they are by showing us pictures of them). It's why people commit adultery when they are away from their families. It's why we have a debt-ridden culture, as people ignore things they can't see (like debts or bankruptcy in the future) in favor of things they can (like fast cars and big houses and trips around the world). Often, it really is a case of out of sight, out of mind.

This is where idolatry comes from. Worshipping an invisible God is very challenging for us as sensual, visual creatures, so throughout history we have tried to get round this by giving our attention and praise to material things. Pagans worshipped the sun and wooden statues; religious people worship icons and crucifixes; secular humanity worships secular humanity by giving the credit for everything good to educated humans, and by literally worshipping celebrities and musicians and footballers. Even the Israelites, the people of God, lost patience while Moses was up on the mountain and built a golden calf, just three months after seeing the Red Sea divided for them, and a few hours after eating the manna that Yahweh had miraculously provided (Ex. 32). Limited, small-minded, physical beings like us want a physical God to worship.

But God is spirit. Or, put negatively, he does not have a body. He does not have physical limitations, such that he can only be in one place at once. He is not constrained by space or even time. The "gods" of other nations in Scripture were always in physical form, limited and finite and visible, so small that they were easily grasped by man. The true God, on the other hand, is "the King of ages, immortal, invisible, the only God" (1 Tim. 1:17), the one "whom no one has ever seen or can see" (1 Tim. 6:16). He is spirit.

Of course, there are a number of times in Scripture when God uses bodily language of himself to help explain what he is like. We call these "anthropomorphisms," pictures of God using human imagery: So we read about God's eyes (his knowledge), his arm (his power to save and to judge), his feet (his rule), his face (his glory), and so on. But we should not take these to mean that God actually has these bodily parts, any more than we would take "the foot of the mountain" to mean something with toes. They are simply word-pictures, given out of God's desire for us to know and understand something of what he is like. God, as Jesus makes clear in John 4:24, is spirit.

That God is spirit, not body, affects our worship, as Jesus explains to the Samaritan woman in this passage. Remember, in the second commandment Yahweh specifically told Israel not to make any likeness of anything—even himself—for use in worship. This is because physical representations of God limit him, since he is spirit. A single physical image cannot possibly convey more than a tiny fraction of the nature of God, and therefore it will distort, rather than reveal, his character, no matter how helpful we might find it.

Think about it. Focusing on a crucifix may help you understand Jesus' suffering humanity, but at the cost of his conquering divinity. Staring at an icon of the Madonna and Child might help you worship the imminent Christ of Matthew 1 and Luke 2, but it will obscure the transcendent Christ of Revelation 1 and Colossians 2, not to mention the transcendent God of Ezekiel 1 and Psalm 2. (Interestingly, when Jesus taught us how we should remember him, he gave us something dynamic—a meal, which focused on both crucifixion and resurrection, trauma and triumph—rather than something static.) So we are to avoid using images, and instead, to worship God "in spirit and in truth," always recognizing that we cannot see him all at once.

The outstanding statement of this, in expounding the same verse we are studying, was made by Stephen Charnock in 1680:

> Since we cannot have a full notion of him, we should endeavor
> to make it as high and as pure as we can … Conceive of him

as excellent, without any imperfection; a Spirit without parts; great without quantity; perfect without quality; everywhere without place; powerful without members; understanding without ignorance; wise without reasoning; light without darkness ... and when you have risen to the highest, conceive him yet infinitely above all you can conceive of spirit, and acknowledge the infirmity of your own minds. And whatsoever conception comes into your minds, say, this is not God; God is more than this: if I could conceive him, he were not God.[1]

Knowing God means acknowledging our limitations. It means resisting the temptation to take a God who is spirit and turn him into a model, or a painting, or anything else we might use to make him more manageable and comprehensible. And it means knowing him and thinking of him as spirit, not body, and worshipping him in spirit and in truth.

Endnote
1. *Stephen Charnock,* The Existence and Attributes of God *(Grand Rapids MI: Baker, 2000), 1: 200–201.*

GOD IS LIGHT

· · · · · ·

In him was life, and the life was the light of men. The light
shines in the darkness, and the darkness has not overcome it.
—John 1:4–5

Most opposites are fairly evenly matched. Take any opposite you can
think of. White doesn't overcome black, nor does black overcome
white, but the two blend together to make gray. Hollywood films
endlessly show us the struggle between good and evil, and although
the good usually wins, it's mostly a pretty fair contest until the end.
Wealth hasn't conquered poverty, and poverty hasn't destroyed wealth.
We could go on: laughter and sorrow, war and peace, disease and medicine. When opposites clash, you cannot be certain which will prevail.

Light is different. No matter how many experiments you perform,
you will never find darkness defeating light. If you flick the light
switch in a dark room, the darkness disappears instantly. No amount

of darkness, not even in pitch-black underground caves, can drown
out the light generated by a small bulb in a head-torch. On a clear
night, a candle on a hilltop can be seen forty-three miles away. Darkness prevails on earth when the sun is not shining on it, but as soon as
it does, the darkness flees. When John says of Jesus, "The light shines
in the darkness, and the darkness has not overcome it," he is stating
the obvious. Of course darkness hasn't overcome light. It can't.

So to say "God is light, and in him is no darkness at all" (1 John 1:5)
is to declare God's invincibility. In whatever context the light picture is
used—and it sometimes means life, sometimes righteousness, and sometimes truth—it speaks of an area where there is no contest. In principle,
it is possible for grace to be overcome by legalism, the holy tainted by the
common, love spoiled by hate. But it is impossible for the light of God to
be drowned out, diluted, or in any way challenged by darkness, any more
than shadows can defeat a halogen lamp. God's light is invincible.

Take truth, for instance. Jesus uses light as a picture for the truth
that he represents:

> And this is the judgment: the light has come into the
> world, and people loved the darkness rather than the
> light because their works were evil. For everyone who
> does wicked things hates the light and does not come
> to the light, lest his works should be exposed. (John
> 3:19–20)

Do you see what he is saying here? If people come into the light,
their wickedness, which they thought was secret, will be revealed for

what it is. Put another way, God's light will always, always overcome their darkness—so they hate the light, and try to hide from it.

You see this all the time. President Nixon tried to keep Watergate secret because he knew that, once it was out, there was no hope for his administration; as soon as people found out what had really happened, further lies would be impossible. The adulterous husband knows that if his wife finds out, there is no turning back, so he lives in ever-increasing secrecy, "lest his works should be exposed." Dictators do not allow freedom of the press. Once the light is on, the darkness cannot survive.

Elsewhere in John's writings, the light metaphor refers to life (John 8:12), and sometimes righteousness (1 John 1:7), but the point is the same. God, who is light, cannot be conquered. He banishes darkness—whether it be secrecy, sin, or death—permanently. If you want to live a life of continued sin and rebellion against God, you need to make sure you hide from him, because your darkness will not be able to withstand his glorious light. On the other hand, if you want life that cannot be overcome even by death, life in all its fullness, then the light of the world is exactly what you need:

> I am the resurrection and the life. Whoever believes in me, though he die, yet shall he live, and everyone who lives and believes in me shall never die. (John 11:25–26)

> When the perishable puts on the imperishable, and the mortal puts on immortality, then shall come to pass the

saying that is written: "Death is swallowed up in victory."
(1 Cor. 15:54)

As light conquers darkness, the resurrection life of Jesus conquers the tomb. Once the life and light of God have broken out in someone, there is nothing Satan himself can do to reinstate the rule and reign of death and darkness.

Falsehood and truth, death and resurrection life, are not evenly matched, nowhere near. When the light appears, the darkness is sent packing forever. This is why an incredibly unlikely claim made by 120 uneducated Jewish people has spread throughout the world (Acts 1:15). It is why the gospel thrives most when it is suppressed. It is also why suggestions that the church will fade are so foolish. God is glorious, permanent, and invincible light. And when the light shines in the darkness, the darkness cannot overcome it.

GOD THE JUDGE

· · · · · ·

For Yahweh is our judge; Yahweh is our lawgiver;
Yahweh is our king; he will save us.
—Isaiah 33:22

There's no pleasing some people. Depending on mood, the same person can attack God for not judging often enough, and then for judging too much. Questions like "How could God allow that evil to continue?" and "How can God say that sleeping with my boyfriend is wrong?" actually contradict each other; one is demanding intervention from God the judge, the other demanding the opposite, like the man who complains that the drug laws are not being enforced and then whines about getting a parking ticket. Such people do not fundamentally have an objection to the idea of God's judgment. They simply differ from him on whether or not they should be on the receiving end of it. The fact that people think like this, always imagining themselves to be the exception to the rule, shows how much we need someone who can "judge with equity," as the psalmists said of Yahweh.

But what does it mean for God to be a judge? In the legal systems of most Western countries, there are five main players, each with different functions. There are politicians, who write the law. There are policemen, who deter people, often by their presence alone, from breaking it, and see that criminals are captured and put on trial. There are jurors, who weigh the evidence and reach a verdict. There is a judge, who interprets the law and passes a sentence, based on the jury's verdict. And there is a prison system, which implements the results of the judge's sentence. To avoid corruption, we prevent any individual from doing more than one of these jobs.

Yahweh, on the other hand, does all five. Look at Isaiah 33:22. Legislating ("our lawgiver"), deterring and punishing ("our king"), deciding and sentencing ("our judge") all are carried out by God himself. Let's consider them each in turn.

First, God the judge writes the law. He alone has authority to say what is allowed and what is not, whether written on tablets of stone or on human hearts by the Spirit (Ezek. 36:26–27). Wonderfully, there can therefore be no misunderstanding or twisting of his commands at a later stage, either by man or by Satan, since he both decrees them and enforces them. As Aslan snaps to the Queen in the film of *The Lion, the Witch and the Wardrobe:* "Do not cite the deep magic to me, Witch. I was there when it was written!"

Next, he deters lawbreaking, by his very presence. Like a policeman who is everywhere, Yahweh restrains evil simply by being there. This is true not only for his disciples; belief in God, however vague or deficient, still acts as a brake on society's slide downhill, which may be why the greatest atrocities committed in the last century went hand in hand with universal atheism. But it is obviously far more true for Christians than others. As Moses told the Israelites, "The fear of Yahweh will be with you to keep you from sinning" (Ex. 20:20 NIV).

Third, God weighs the evidence and reaches a verdict. In human trials, even the guilty can get off (and the innocent get convicted) because of anomalies in the evidence, the relative skill of the lawyers, and the fallibility of the jury. Not so with God the judge. No mafia chieftain or spin doctor can bribe or talk his way out of anything before God. Have you ever tried to impress your friends by pretending to be knowledgeable about something, and then found out that there was a genuine expert in the room? I have, and when you get discovered, there's a crushing feeling of exposure and humiliation, as everyone watches your act crumble before them, and sees you as the rather pathetic show-off you really are. The rich and powerful in this world will discover that when they stand under the all-knowing gaze of Jesus Christ. How could anyone fool an omniscient God?

Fourth, God the judge passes the sentence. This is actually what Judgment Day is for. Many of us think of Judgment Day as a trial, a time when evidence will be heard and a verdict given, but it is not that. God already knows all the evidence, and the verdict of guilty has already been given. The sentence on our lives simply depends on whether we have accepted Jesus' taking of the guilty verdict on our behalf, so that we are declared righteous—called "justification by faith"—or not. More poetically:

And I saw the dead, great and small, standing before the throne, and books were opened. Then another book was opened, which is the book of life. And the dead were judged by what was written in the books, according to what they had done ... And if anyone's name was not found written in the book of life, he was thrown into the lake of fire. (Rev. 20:12, 15)

Finally, God the judge implements the results of his own sentence. This is not simply a question of heaven and hell, although it is that, but also of rewards (and punishments) that correspond with the way we have lived: a crown, treasures in heaven, rest, inheritance, rewards, promises, a rich welcome, responsibility in the age to come, and so on. For those of us who have lived in the light of eternity, Judgment Day will be a day of celebration, not terror. The plaintiff on the verge of being awarded massive damages does not dread Judgment Day; they can't sleep for excitement, wondering what might be in store.

Legislator, deterrent, jury, judge, and executioner: Yahweh is all of them at once. Or, in Isaiah's words, "Yahweh is our judge; Yahweh is our lawgiver; Yahweh is our king; he will save us."

GOD IS LOVE

. . . . . .

Anyone who does not love does not know God, because God is love.
In this the love of God was made manifest among us, that God
sent his only Son into the world, so that we might live through
him. In this is love, not that we have loved God, but that he
loved us and sent his Son to be the propitiation for our sins.
—1 John 4:8–10

Describing the love of God is like trying to tackle a pool table. You can give it your best shot, but ultimately it is far too big for you to get your arms round, so any attempt you make will be hopelessly limited. There is so much that we could say about the love of God—and the even more amazing truth that God *is* love—that in this reflection we will restrict ourselves to looking at what John says about it here. In these three beautiful verses, John points out the love of God in his identity ("God is love"), in his incarnation ("God sent his only Son into the world"), and in his initiation of relationship with us ("not that we have loved God, but that he loved us"). Each is powerful and moving.

Come with me back in time, to before the foundation of the world. There is no sky, no earth, no cornflakes, and certainly no you. How can God have been love then? What else was there to love? We would be incapable of love in such a situation, but John informs us here that love is something God *is,* not just something he *does.* So who or what was he loving? John 17:24 provides the answer:

> Father, I desire that they also, whom you have given me, may be with me where I am, to see my glory that you have given me *because you loved me before the foundation of the world.*

God was loving God! Before anything existed, there was a loving community in the Godhead, with each of the members of the Trinity loving one another. The Father, when faced with the radiance and perfection of the Son, could have no other reaction than love. The Spirit, watching the compassion and might of the Father, could likewise not respond with anything but deep affection. God does not just love sometimes, or even all the time; he is love, so much so that anyone who doesn't love doesn't even know him.

Now come to a cowshed in the Middle East in 4 BC. Love is not a fuzzy feeling, but a self-giving commitment that results in action, and here we are going to get an example of what that involved. It involved sending the Son, from his position in heavenly glory and sinless perfection, to earth, to become flesh. You know the shock your body gets when you jump from a hot tub into an icy pool? (If you don't, try it sometime.) Now imagine going from a place where there was no sin at all, to a place like Bethlehem, or Jerusalem, or London for that matter. It involved the Son laying aside his majesty and becoming an infant who fell over and vomited and soiled his nappy and grazed his knees. It involved walking a mile in our shoes, facing temptation of all kinds, misunderstanding, bereavement, and rejection. "In this the love of God was made manifest among us, that God sent his only Son into the world, so that we might live through him" (1 John 4:9).

Now come with me about ten miles north of there, to a rubbish dump outside Jerusalem, thirty-three years later. Much has changed. The infant, the most powerful symbol of the love of God that could ever have been given, has grown up into a man, but a man no longer physically recognizable because of the welts on his face and the ripped flesh across his chest and back. The sky above him no longer has bright stars in the night, but dark clouds in the day. The two people next to him are not loving parents, but common criminals; the crowds have changed from saying, "Hosanna in the highest" to "His blood be upon us and our children." His earthly father has died. His closest friends have abandoned, denied, or betrayed him. His enemies have mocked and humiliated him. The government has stripped, tortured, and crucified him. And the wrath of God at all our lies and lusts and pride and envy and greed is being poured out on him, breaking utterly the fellowship with the Father and the Spirit that he has experienced and exulted in since before the foundation of the world.

If that doesn't explain to you what the love of God is, come closer to the cross, and listen to what Jesus is saying. The only one who matters is thinking of his mother, his friend, and even the criminal next to him. The God who created water is asking for a drink. The God-man whose presence had never borne any sin is crying out in anguish at being forsaken by his Father. The man with nails through his wrists and feet, his lungs slowly filling with his own blood, is crying out, "Father, forgive them, for they know not what they do." Astoundingly, the one who decided to allow man to make his own choices, now fully experiencing their consequences, is shouting triumphantly that those consequences have been dealt with, finished—a victory cry that still resounds across history, affirming once and for all that the love of God is a love of both power and passion, both perfection and propitiation.

"In this is love, not that we have loved God, but that he loved us and sent his Son to be the propitiation for our sins." Amen and amen.

 STOP AND STUDY

It is profoundly upbuilding to study the love of God, even if sometimes it can be a bit mind-bending. Here are a few suggestions that will help you grapple with what the Bible says about God's love. But be warned: They may change your way of thinking!

D. A. Carson, *The Difficult Doctrine of the Love of God* (Wheaton IL: Crossway, 2000).
—A brief, but fairly in-depth study of how we fit together the love of God with his sovereignty, suffering, and so on.

John Piper, "The Goal of God's Love May Not Be What You Think It Is," first published in the *Dallas Morning News*, and available free by searching at www.desiringgod.org/resourcelibrary.
—A superb and quite mind-bending take on what God is most passionate about.

C. H. Spurgeon, "Herein Is Love," preached January 19, 1896, and available free at www.spurgeon.org/sermons/2448.htm.
—A classic exposition of 1 John 4 from the "prince of preachers."

Philip Yancey, *What's So Amazing About Grace?* (Grand Rapids, MI: Zondervan, 1997).

—One of the best Christian books you will ever read, if you haven't already; a powerful and often moving challenge to understand, and live, the love and grace of Jesus.

A. W. Tozer, *The Knowledge of the Holy* (New York: HarperOne, 1998; Milton Keynes: Authentic, 1994), 118–25.

—Tozer's sweeping vision of God will inspire you, and his chapter on love is extremely helpful.

GOD IS UNCHANGEABLE

• • • • • •

Of old you laid the foundation of the earth, and the heavens are the
work of your hands. They will perish, but you will remain; they will
all wear out like a garment. You will change them like a robe, and they
will pass away, but you are the same, and your years have no end.
—Psalm 102:25–27

Try sitting completely still. You are not allowed to move anything
except your eyes. Ready?

Almost everything about you is changing right now, even as you
sit completely still. Your body is changing, as every second you produce
twenty-five million cells, and your brain processes one hundred million new pieces of information. Your location is changing at a rate of
sixty-six thousand miles per hour, along with the rest of the large lump
of rock we call the earth. This rock is itself changing all the time, with
the earth's crust moving continuously, continents changing shape, and

Mount Everest growing five centimeters every year. The sun, probably the largest and most steady object you know anything about, is changing rather more dramatically: It is now fifty million tons lighter than it was when you started reading this paragraph. Everything changes.

Except God. The psalmist who wrote the verses above did not know any of these facts, but he knew that everything in creation was changeable. So he took the most steady and certain things there are in life—the foundation of the earth, and the sky—and made a comparison between them and Almighty God. The earth's crust isn't permanent; it will wear out like a pair of school trousers. The sky won't be there forever; God will change it like you change your shoes. Yahweh, on the other hand, is always the same. He will remain the same forever, and his years have no end.

It's just as well. If God could change, there would be trouble. What if he changed for the worse? He would no longer be perfect. All right, so what if he changed for the better? Then he would not have been perfect in the first place. If God changed in any way, it would leave us with a problem.

Besides, God has taken great care in his book to show us that he doesn't change. He puts it bluntly in Malachi 3:6—"I Yahweh do not change." James, who can always be relied upon to tell it like it is, talks about God as "the Father of lights with whom there is no variation or shadow due to change" (James 1:17). And Hebrews 13:8 tells us that "Jesus Christ is the same yesterday and today and forever." The Bible is crystal clear: God, unlike everything else in the universe, never changes.

The last of these verses is particularly striking. It comes at the end of a book, Hebrews, which has been devoted to showing that even the most fixed things in Judaism were always destined to be temporary. This doesn't mean much to us, but these things had been in place for fourteen hundred years—in our terms, the law was twice as old then as the English language is now. Yet Hebrews says the law is only "a shadow." The old covenant is "obsolete and growing old." Gifts and sacrifices are just "regulations for the body imposed until the time of reformation." The commandment "is set aside because of its weakness and uselessness." All the foundations of the Jewish way of life, Hebrews says, are changeable. Only Jesus is the same yesterday and today and for ever.

This has massive implications for our lives. A. W. Tozer comments,

> What peace it brings to the Christian's heart to realize that our Heavenly Father never differs from Himself. In coming to Him at any time we need not wonder whether we shall find Him in a receptive mood. He is always receptive to misery and need, as well as to love and faith. He does not keep office hours nor set aside periods when He will see no one. Neither does He change His mind about anything. Today, this moment, He feels toward His creatures, toward babies, toward the sick, the fallen, the sinful, exactly as He did when He sent His only begotten Son into the world to die for mankind.[1]

This should give us such confidence in approaching God. His commitment to his glory, his compassion for the broken, his anger at sin, and his passion for justice remain constant. So when we come to God, there are no banana skins to slip on, no nasty surprises we might find. He is always the same.

God's unchangeableness is unique. It is what theologians call an "incommunicable attribute" of God, which means something about him that is not shared by anyone else. Everything else, without exception, changes: plants and animals and governments and scientific theories and galaxies and mountains and empires.

But God never does.

Endnote
1. *A. W. Tozer,* The Knowledge of the Holy *(New York: HarperOne, 1998; Milton Keynes: Authentic, 2005), 63–64.*

GOD IS FAITHFUL AND TRUE

· · · · · ·

What if some did not have faith? Will their lack of faith nullify God's
faithfulness? Not at all! Let God be true, and every man a liar.
—*Romans 3:3–4 NIV*

Have you ever wondered whether God was truthful or not? Has anything ever happened to you that made you question his faithfulness? If
so, take a minute to think about this puzzle.

Three friends have a meal in a restaurant. The waiter arrives with
the bill, which is thirty dollars, and the friends put in ten dollars
each to cover it. When the waiter leaves the table, he finds that he has
overcharged them—the bill for the meal should have been twenty-
five dollars—so he finds five one-dollar bills in change. Now, being
a slightly dishonest waiter, he decides to give the friends one dollar
each, so they end up paying twenty-seven dollars between them, and
he pockets the remaining two dollars. But twenty-seven dollars plus

two dollars equals twenty-nine dollars, not thirty. Where has the extra dollar gone?[1]

When my wife and I first heard that puzzle, our responses were very different. Rachel got so confused that she ended up announcing there was a mathematical mistake! She spoke to lots of people, and none of them could solve it, so she concluded that there was a flaw in arithmetic; in some circumstances, perhaps one plus one does not always equal two. (I think she was joking.) I did the opposite. Whatever the numbers were, I knew there could not possibly be a mistake. So I admitted that there must be a logical solution, but that I just didn't understand the numbers well enough—I must have made a mistake somewhere. My confidence in the mathematics was greater than my confidence in my own ability to figure out the answer correctly.

This is the way Paul thinks about the truthfulness of God in Romans 3. In writing the letter, he is faced with a problem: the fact that some Jews have not believed in Jesus, which makes it look like God's promise to Abraham has been broken. One conclusion people might come to, based on this, is that God is not true, not faithful, after all. But Paul utterly dismisses this as impossible, exclaiming, "Not at all!" No matter what has happened, no matter what it looks like, the one thing that cannot be true is that God is unfaithful. For God to be unfaithful would be the equivalent of there being a mistake in arithmetic.

The phrase he uses is remarkable: "Let God be true, and every man a liar." What does this slightly strange phrase mean? Well, let's say God says one thing, and every person who has ever lived says the opposite. Who are you going to believe? Paul's point is that, even if every person in history lined up and said God had done something unfaithful, he still would not believe them. God is so true, so faithful, so righteous in all his ways, that even if every expert through the ages agreed he had been wrong, it would only show that, like with our thirty-dollar puzzle, people had made a mistake somewhere.

For Paul, this is a reflex. When I put my hand on the cooker yesterday, it jumped off it again before I had even realized that it was painful, because I have a reflex, an automatic response that happens without me processing it. (It is just as well, because if moving my hand depended on me working it out, I would have badly damaged myself by the time I had.) Paul's reaction is like this. When asked whether God might have been unfaithful, his answer is immediate: "Not a chance!" Notice that he has not yet explained why, despite Israel's lack of faith, God is true. (It is just as well, because if God's truth depended on our working everything out, we would badly damage ourselves by the time we had.) In fact, Paul doesn't go into any detail on this issue for another six chapters. Even so, before he does, he wants his readers to be completely clear. There is no way, under any circumstances, regardless of what anyone and everyone might say or do, that God has done anything wrong, false, misleading, or unfaithful.

Ultimately, Paul argues in chapters 9 to 11, there is an explanation for the unbelief of Israel—God's free and sovereign choice, and his passion for his glory—just like there is an explanation for whatever you feel angry or frustrated with God for. But if you don't have an explanation yet, what do you do in the meantime? Some people take the "jury's out" approach: God may or may not be faithful, depending on whether I can get my mind round what he's done. This is as absurd as spending the time before you understand the puzzle wondering whether there is a mistake in math. But others, like Paul, acknowledge the limitations of their understanding, and simply affirm that no matter what has happened, God is still faithful.

In other words: "Let God be true, and every man a liar."

Endnote

1. Since first publishing this book, a number of readers have commented that they couldn't continue reading until they had worked out the solution (although none of them, to be fair, thought in the meantime there was a mathematical error). The numbers were never supposed to add up to $30, but to $25, since that is the total amount added to the till. And $9 + $9 + $9 - $2 = $25.

God Is Holy

· · · · · ·

In the year that King Uzziah died I saw the Lord sitting upon
a throne, high and lifted up; and the train of his robe filled the
temple. Above him stood the seraphim. Each had six wings: with
two he covered his face, and with two he covered his feet, and
with two he flew. And one called to another and said, "Holy, holy,
holy is Yahweh of hosts; the whole earth is full of his glory!"
—Isaiah 6:1–3

Perhaps the most central truth about God is that he is holy. Ask a semi-
nary student, and she might say "omnipotence" or "providence"; ask
the average Joe on the street, and he would probably reply "love." But
if you asked the angels, who dwell in his presence, they would say one
thing: "Holy, holy, holy is Yahweh of hosts." The two occasions when
we hear what the angels are saying in Scripture are separated by eight
hundred years (here and in Revelation 4), but they are saying exactly

the same thing in both, so overwhelmed are they by the staggering holiness of God. Presumably, they have been saying it ever since, and are saying it right now.

Holiness means "otherness." To say that God is holy is to say that he is other than you, separate from you, distinct, cut off, set apart, devoted to himself and nothing else. It is this feature of God that is so apparent when we get those open heaven scenes in the Bible: the utter difference between him and everything else. Isaiah, who is so undone by seeing the holiness of God that he calls down woes on himself, gives us here a few ways in which God is totally unlike us. Let's reflect on them.

The chapter opens with: "In the year that King Uzziah died I saw the Lord." This is one of the most obvious contrasts between Yahweh and us: We die, and he doesn't. King Uzziah, king of Israel during a period of remarkable prosperity, had just died, but Yahweh was still living. Our life is contingent upon food, water, oxygen, and so on, but he is independent, with life in himself, and no need of being provided for or served by anyone or anything (Acts 17:25). Everything else in the universe is finite, with either a beginning and an end (like animals), or a beginning but no end (like the souls of people and angels). God alone is eternal:

"The eternal God is your dwelling place, and underneath are the everlasting arms" (Deut. 33:27).

"I am the Alpha and the Omega, the first and the last, the beginning and the end" (Rev. 22:13).

Another vast difference between God and us is that he is "sitting upon a throne." His sovereignty is so unchallenged that he can be seated, and yet still governing the whole of creation. When I have responsibilities, however small, I rush around the whole time, trying to ensure they don't get on top of me; and the bigger they are, the more frenetic I become. Yet God, with all things under his control and the responsibility for feeding the sparrows and sustaining the stars, is "sitting upon a throne." Because his word is so powerful, and his authority so sweeping, he need never panic, rush, or even worry. He, unlike us, is in complete control.

Next is the wonderful phrase: "high and lifted up." Height is another way Scripture shows the difference between us and Yahweh: his throne is in the skies (Ps. 103:19), and he rides on the clouds (Ps. 104:3). When the rulers of the earth plot to overthrow God's kingdom, "He who sits in the heavens laughs" (Ps. 2:4). When man makes his smug but very lame attempt to build a tower that would reach the heavens, there is more than a hint of sarcasm in the phrase, "and Yahweh came down to see the city and the tower, which the children of man had built" (Gen. 11:5). It is no coincidence that God frequently appears to man on mountains, as it shows us how "other" than us he is—if you or I were picked up now and put at the summit of Mount Everest, the reason we would die so quickly is because of its otherness, the difference between the mountain and our normal conditions. It is the same with the mountain of God, the mere touching of which resulted in death (Ex. 19:13). Yahweh, more than we can conceive, is "high and lifted up."

We are then told that "the train of his robe filled the temple." Traditionally, when a bride enters a church, she has a train to her dress, which may be several yards long. Imagine being at a wedding, though, where the train of the dress is so long that as she walks up the aisle, it keeps coming and coming, so that people start having to be moved to make room for it, and eventually the entire church has to be evacuated because the train fills the building. That is the picture here. It suggests an extravagance, a resplendence, to God's presence that is unthinkably unlike ours.

We could go on, but one final thing that leaps off the page is how intensely unapproachable God is to those who are not holy. The angels, as we consider in the reflection "Yahweh of Hosts," couldn't even look at him. Isaiah does, and immediately realizes what a terrifying place that is to be (6:5). He may well have had in his mind the various people who had been killed by God for approaching him without due consideration for his holiness. Offering unauthorized fire (Lev. 10:2), touching the ark of the covenant (2 Sam. 6:7), and even looking at it (1 Sam. 6:19), were all things that had resulted in immediate death to Israelites. Daringly, a church I attended once preached about all the people God killed in Scripture. As the revelation of God's holiness dawned on the congregation, their reactions changed from "Why him?" to "Why not us?" This is the sort of concept of Yahweh's holiness that Isaiah has here.

The living God, sitting on a throne, high and lifted up, resplendent and unapproachable—this is a small part of what the angels can see all the time. It is no surprise, therefore, that as Revelation 4:8 puts it, "day and night they never cease to say" how holy their God is.

# WAIT AND WORSHIP

When you come face to face with the holiness of Yahweh, you can't help singing about him. In fact, that's something that Scripture urges us to do (the word "sing" appears seventy times in Psalms alone!). So it is worth finding good songs about God's holiness, and learning to sing them. This hymn, written by Reginald Heber in 1826, is an excellent way of responding to our holy God.

Holy, holy, holy! Lord God Almighty!
Early in the morning our song shall rise to thee.
Holy, holy, holy! Merciful and mighty,
God in three persons, blessed Trinity!

Holy, holy, holy! All the saints adore thee,
Casting down their golden crowns around the glassy sea;
Cherubim and seraphim falling down before thee,
Which were, and are, and evermore shall be.

Holy, holy, holy! Though the darkness hide thee,
Though the eye of sinful man thy glory may not see,

Only thou art holy; there is none beside thee,
Perfect in power, in love and purity.

Holy, holy, holy! Lord God Almighty!
All thy works shall praise thy name, in earth and sky and sea.
Holy, holy, holy! Merciful and mighty,
God in three persons, blessed Trinity.

As well as the hymns, there have been a number of superb new songs written in the last few years on the subject of God's holiness. Each is worth downloading from iTunes or buying on CD:

"Holy, Holy" by Nathan Fellingham, © 1994 Thankyou Music.

"Agnus Dei" by Michael W. Smith, © 1990 Milene Music.

"Facedown" by Matt Redman, © 2004 Thankyou Music.

"Holy Is the Lord God Almighty" by Chris Tomlin and Louie Giglio, © 2003 worshiptogether.com Songs/sixsteps Music/EMI CMG.

"Be Lifted Up" by Paul Oakley, © 2003 Thankyou Music.

......

EXPLORATION II
The Names of God

......

GOD

· · · · · ·

Be still, and know that I am God. I will be exalted
among the nations, I will be exalted in the earth!
—Psalm 46:10

Every language known to me has a word for "god." Some languages
don't have any tenses, or a word for "have," or even "the," but all have
a word for "god." They may not be talking about the same god, or the
true God, but they all have the word. Somewhere in the mind-set of
everyone in the world is the idea of a god.

"God" is not really a name, actually, but a title. It is what we call a
common noun, not a proper noun—it is like referring to "the president"
rather than "George Washington." This means, of course, that the word
"god" can be understood in lots of different ways, depending on people's
backgrounds. This is why the Bible writers often refer to, for instance,
"the God of Abraham, Isaac, and Jacob"; it identifies which god they are

talking about. If I use the term "the president" in France, Burundi, and Nicaragua, it will be understood as referring to three different people.

There is an exception to this principle. Imagine I was trying to say that France was the greatest country in the world, so there was really only one president, and all other so-called "presidents" were nothing in comparison. Under those circumstances, I might speak of "the president" as a way of making a point: that our president is the only one who really matters. We actually get quite close to this today. It is common to hear someone say simply "the president" to refer to the American one, even though there are hundreds of presidents in the world. This is because one of them is vastly more powerful and significant than the others.

When the Old Testament writers refer to "God," they are making a point like this. They are saying there is only one God, and all the gods of the nations are pathetic parodies, contrived copies, of the real one. There is far more difference in power and importance between God and "the gods of the nations" than there is between the president of the United States and the president of the Chipping Sodbury Croquet Club. One is, in fact, nothing more than a parody—a rather silly looking copy—of the other.

Now imagine the U.S. president called a colossal press conference, went on television to talk to the world, and said, "Be still and know that I am the president. I will be exalted among the nations." Suddenly, a title that has never bothered anyone much would sound deeply controversial, striking, and offensive. It would be a claim to absolute authority in the world, a claim that other presidents were not just inferior but also insignificant and impotent, and that this would soon be acknowledged throughout the earth. Effectively, a statement like this would redefine the word "president."

This, of course, is exactly what God and his prophets do throughout the Old Testament. There is no need to speak of a sun god, a moon god, a fertility god, a god of war, and so on. There is just God. He is so different from the gods of the nations that they should not be put in the same sentence. He is given no introduction in Genesis 1, no explanation anywhere in Scripture, and he does not try to explain himself in Psalm 46. He just says, "Be still, and know that I am God."

In some languages, the word for god may mean just the idol that the people pray to. This is what Paul found in Athens in Acts 17; the problem wasn't that people didn't believe in God, it was that they had no idea what he was like. In Western culture, as much as anywhere, when people use the word "god," they often mean someone or something totally unlike the God of the Bible. Try this experiment: Next time people tell you that they don't believe in God, ask them to describe which god they don't believe in. The odds are, when they've gotten over their surprise at your question, they will vaguely describe a distant, randomly interfering, impersonal being, who made the world a long time ago and has not done much since. You will then be able to double their surprise by cheerfully informing them that you don't believe in that god either.

So people use the word "god" in a lot of different ways. The Hebrew word *Elohim* used in the Bible, though, does not mean "a god" or "gods," but simply "God," the creator of heaven and earth, the God of Abraham, Isaac, and Jacob, the one who claims absolute authority for himself, and the one who will be exalted among the nations and in the earth. So be still and know him!

YAHWEH

• • • • • •

God spoke to Moses and said to him, "I am Yahweh. I appeared
to Abraham, to Isaac, and to Jacob, as God Almighty, but by
my name Yahweh I did not make myself known to them."
—Exodus 6:2–3

God has a name. In fact, he has hundreds of names, but one in particular. Over sixty-eight hundred times in the Old Testament, God is referred to by this name, a name that speaks of personality and relationship and covenant and eternity. That name in Hebrew is the four letters YHWH, translated "the LORD" in many English Bibles, and was probably pronounced "Yahweh" originally, although you may have heard it as "Jehovah." It is the name of God.

Why does God have a name? Well, names achieve three things. First, they help us identify people, and this is the main reason we use names today. Names tell people apart in a very crowded world; there are lots of people, so we use names to tell who is who. In the time of the Old Testament, there were lots of gods worshipped by other nations, like Dagon, Baal, Bel, Nebo, Molech, Asherah, and a number of others. The name Yahweh identified the God of Israel as opposed to the others.

Another thing names do is help establish personal relationships. In almost every culture, the first thing you do when you meet someone is tell her your name and find out hers. At the other end of the scale, have you ever felt insulted when you meet someone several times, and then discover he can't remember your name? Or felt good when an important person who you didn't think had noticed you called you by your name? Names are a very important part of human relationships. They act as a sort of indicator of intimacy (so my dad gets called "Sir" by his tailor, "Mr. Wilson" by his clients, "Charles" by his business partner, and "Charlie" by his family.) In revealing his name to Moses, Yahweh put himself into the most intimate relationship available with Moses. Astonishingly, he does the same with us.

A third thing names do in the Bible is to show something of people's character. In English, most of our first names have no meaning, so we don't grasp this easily. In the Bible, though, names are often very significant, and can reveal God's view of a person. In Genesis 17:5, Yahweh starts calling Abram (which means "exalted father") by a new name, Abraham ("father of many nations"), to back up his promise to him. In Genesis 32:28, after a long wrestling match, Yahweh takes Jacob ("twister," "supplanter," "wheeler and dealer") and changes his name to Israel ("he struggles with God"). Maybe the most famous example is Peter, because of Jesus' words in Matthew 16:18—"you are

Peter (*petros*), and on this rock (*petra*) I will build my church." As the evangelist J. John puts it, "Jesus looked at the ground and saw this big boulder lying there. He looked at Peter. He looked at the boulder. He saw the resemblance. He called him Rocky."[1]

God's names show his character too. And this is what God is doing in the verse we started with. We know this because the name itself, "Yahweh," had been first used way back in Genesis 2. People used it from the time of Enosh onward. Abraham used it. In Exodus 6 itself, we are told that Moses' mother's name is Jochebed ("Yahweh is glory"). So God cannot be introducing Moses to the word for the first time ever. Instead, he is revealing his character to Moses in a way he never had to Abraham, Isaac, and Jacob. He is changing the way people think about him, from that of an office to that of a person.

The name "Yahweh" is most likely based on the name "I am who I am" in Exodus 3:14, which we discuss in the next reflection. So we could give an English version of "Yahweh" as something like "eternal," or "always." But to the Hebrews, the name itself, and everything it stood for, was seen as being incredibly holy. It was so sacred to them they never even pronounced it out loud, replacing it with *Adonai* (Lord) when they read Scripture. On this, the Bible teacher Martyn Lloyd-Jones comments,

> More and more, as I consider these things, and spend ever-increasing time in reading my Bible, I understand why the ancient Jews never mentioned the name Jehovah. They were filled with such a sense of awe and reverence, they had such a conception of the majesty of God, that in

a sense they dared not even utter the name. I much prefer that, to hearing people saying "Dear God." I do not find such an expression in the Bible. I do find "Holy Father," but never "Dear God."[2]

Revealing the name Yahweh to us shows God's desire for relationship with us and lets us know something of his character. But it ought also to make us stand in awe. As Yahweh said to Moses in Exodus 3:5: "Take your sandals off your feet, for the place on which you are standing is holy ground."

Endnotes
1. *J. John, speaking at Lee Abbey in 1989.*
2. *D. Martyn Lloyd-Jones,* God the Father, God the Son *(Wheaton, IL: Good News Publishers, 1996; London: Hodder & Stoughton, 1996), 52–53.*

I AM WHO I AM

• • • • • •

*Then Moses said to God, "If I come to the people of Israel and
say to them, 'The God of your fathers has sent me to you,' and
they ask me, 'What is his name?' what shall I say to them?"
God said to Moses, "I AM WHO I AM." And he said, "Say
this to the people of Israel, 'I AM has sent me to you.'"*
—Exodus 3:13–14

Moses is terrified. He is standing opposite a burning bush that is
somehow not being burnt up, confronted with the living God himself. Not surprisingly, he is hiding his face in fear, cowering in terror,
just from hearing God's voice. But worse is to come, because God
has a job for him.

Moses fled Egypt forty years ago because he murdered someone,
and the world's most powerful man was trying to kill him. Now he
has to go back to the same country, back to the world's most powerful

man, and tell him that his slaves are to go free. This order is as ridiculous as telling the president of America that his country is no longer allowed to use oil, or the Internet—the entire economy depends on it. The difference is, Pharaoh could punish Moses without being bound by the same human rights laws! So Moses is a little bit scared. In desperation, he asks God for his name.

God's reply is simple: "I am who I am" (or "I will be what I will be"). This is not a one-off name God plucks off the shelf to respond to a situation. It is the most likely basis for the name "Yahweh," which is used sixty-eight hundred times in Scripture (Yahweh and the Hebrew word for "to be," *hayah*, sound very similar, and the two names are used in parallel in Exodus 3:14–15). What a name! Of all the things God could call himself, he chooses "I am."

The name "I am," quite simply, shows that God is. It reminds Moses that, no matter how powerful Pharaoh is, he has a God who actually exists, in contrast to the Egyptian "gods." The great "I am" then demonstrates his existence with action, in a series of devastating plagues on Egypt. As the Egyptian gods are time and again shown powerless to protect the nation from blood, frogs, gnats, flies, plague, boils, hail, locusts, and darkness, you can see the massive, terrible contrast between the "I am" and the "they are not." The final judgment, the death of the firstborn, says "I am" so clearly to Pharaoh that he lets the Israelites go. Moses, though weak, overcomes the world's most powerful man. He has the "I am," the real God, on his side.

Now, God existing may not seem that controversial. Many of your friends probably agree that God exists, even if they are not disciples of Jesus. The problem is, if you read on in the story, that you'll find

Pharaoh believed in God (Ex. 8:8). Hitler probably believed in God. James 2:19 says that even the demons believe there is one God, and shudder. So believing that God exists is not enough.

You see, the name "I am" means more than just that God exists. It means he matters. When Moses says, "Who am I?" God shows him that it is irrelevant, because he has the "I am" on his side, and that is what matters. Remember, Moses already believes in God, but God doesn't want this on the edge of Moses' thinking. He wants it smack-dab in the center.

I'm sure you learned at school that the air we breathe is almost all made up of nitrogen (80 percent) and oxygen (20 percent).[1] If I asked you if you believed in nitrogen, you would certainly say yes. But if I asked how nitrogen affected your life, you would probably admit that it made no difference. You would believe it was there, but you would never have thought about it or even particularly wanted it, and it certainly would not affect your decisions. Oxygen is a different story, though. You would believe in it, but you would also know how dependent you are on it: to breathe, to burn fuel, and so on. You would know how difficult life is without enough oxygen, and it would drive all sorts of your decisions, from holding your breath underwater to using an asthma inhaler to preserving the rainforests.

Most people are "nitrogen believers" in God. They believe he is there, but they never acknowledge their need of him or let him influence their thinking. They certainly don't make decisions with reference to him. Believing in God is not enough. To be a disciple is to be an oxygen believer: someone who realizes how earth-shakingly important God is, how much he matters in every way, how he is the "I am."

So God revealed himself to Moses, and to us, as the "I am." Isn't
that amazing? If I were God, I would go for something more apparently
dramatic: "Superpower," or "Blazing One," or "Cosmos Creator." But
he goes for "I am who I am." Right at the center of our understanding
of his character, God wanted us to know he always was, he always will
be, and he matters. So he made it his name.

Endnote
*1. This illustration is adapted from a sermon by John Piper, at Bethlehem Baptist Church,
Minneapolis in 1984.*

YAHWEH-WILL-PROVIDE

• • • • • •

And Abraham lifted up his eyes and looked, and behold, behind him
was a ram, caught in a thicket by his horns. And Abraham went and
took the ram and offered it up as a burnt offering instead of his son.
So Abraham called the name of that place, "Yahweh-will-provide."
—Genesis 22:13–14

You will probably never be told to kill your own child. I imagine it
is just about the worst thing anyone could ever have to do, the sort
of thing that only ever happens in nightmares. In Abraham's case, it
was arguably worse than normal, because his son Isaac was the one he
had been waiting for, the miracle child, the child of promise, the one
through whom the whole world would be blessed. Yet here is Abraham,
up a mountain in Palestine in 1800 BC, tying his son down to an altar
and preparing to sacrifice him. He is about to kill his only son.

    If we stop the story there, it is pretty remarkable. What would you

do if you heard God tell you to kill your child? You would probably
ignore it, telling yourself that it could not possibly be God, because
God is loving, God would never tell you to kill someone, and God
would never undermine his promise. Abraham, however, knows God's
voice, and obeys. Even when his boy asks him the heart-wrenching
question, "Where is the lamb for a burnt offering?," Abraham is utterly
confident in God. His reply, "God will provide for himself a lamb for a
burnt offering," shows how well he knows God. Abraham has learned
through experience that God always provides, even when it is impossible. So what happens? An angel calls out to him, Abraham looks,
and there is a ram caught in a thicket, which he then offers instead of
Isaac. Abraham was right to be confident in God's provision, and so he
names the place accordingly: "Yahweh-will-provide."

This is one of eight places in the Bible where God reveals a compound name to people. That means God adds something to the name
Yahweh to make a longer name, *Yahweh-yireh,* or "Yahweh-will-
provide." It would be like calling your local mechanic "Tony-fix-it":
The name is a summary of what the person is and does. So Yahweh-
will-provide is a name for God.

You see, providing is part of God's nature. It is not just something
he does, it is part of who he is—that's why it is his name. God cannot
be anything other than a provider. He will always provide, wherever
he is, and whatever situation we are in. He does this because he always
knows what we need well before we do. Think about it: The ram was
in the thicket already! God knew Abraham would need it, and had
already made provision for him.

In fact, both the English and Hebrew words here have the sense of "seeing." Our word "provide" is made up of two parts: "pro" (meaning before, as in "proactive") and "vide" (meaning see, as in "video"). The Hebrew word *yireh* is similar, and carries the sense of "seeing to" something. God always sees what we are going to need before we get there, and so he sees to it, by providing for us in advance. Or, as one Bible teacher puts it,

> God stood at the beginning of history and saw everything as though it were present. And he saw to everything he saw. There wasn't a thing God saw he didn't see to, so we don't need to get worried about what we can see, because God already saw it and saw to it![1]

There are two things about God's provision in this story that I have seen repeated time and again in everyday life. One is that God often waits until the last possible moment before providing for us. This is not just for fun; he does it to teach us to rely on him completely. What if Abraham had found the ram on the way up the mountain, long before the sacrifice? His confidence in God's provision would not have been nearly so great, and he might even have dismissed it as a coincidence (does that ring any bells?). So God waits until we are utterly dependent, until we have no source but him, and then comes through for us.

Secondly, God often gives to us as we give to him. As Abraham gave up his most precious possession, his son, God gave back to him. In my life, God has frequently given miraculously just after I have given something valuable away myself. Did you know that God challenges us to test him on this one? In Malachi 3:10, God says, "Bring the full tithe into the storehouse, that there may be food in my house. And thereby put me to the test, says Yahweh of hosts, if I will not open the windows of heaven for you and pour down for you a blessing until there is no more need."

God tells us to test him, to see if he will provide for us when we give to him. What an invitation! How can we out-give God?

The answer is, of course, we can't, because he is Yahweh-will-provide. As Abraham found out.

Endnote
1. *Judson Cornwall, speaking on* God's Excellent Name *at Malvern in 1988.*

YAHWEH-YOUR-HEALER

• • • • • •

*If you will diligently listen to the voice of Yahweh your God, and
do that which is right in his eyes, and give ear to his commandments and keep all his statutes, I will put none of the diseases on
you that I put on the Egyptians, for I am Yahweh-your-healer.*
—Exodus 15:26

God heals. If you read the Bible, this is obvious. In both Old and New
Testaments, we read about blind people seeing, barren women giving
birth, deaf people hearing, and lame people walking. We read about
the healing of people with internal bleeding and epilepsy and snake
bites and sliced-off ears and paralysis and skin diseases and dumbness
and fevers and dysentery. We see demons being cast out, and even the
dead being raised on several occasions. The prophets healed people,
Jesus healed people, and the early church healed people. Throughout

Scripture, we see people with serious physical sicknesses encounter God, and walk away completely free. God is a healing God.

Some people today are not so sure about this, saying that this may have happened in the past, but it no longer happens now. You may have noticed that God the healer rarely comes up in systematic theology books. You may also have come across all sorts of (rather confusing) debates about the timing of the kingdom, the end of the apostolic age, and the evidence for healing through church history. But all these debates, although not wrong in themselves, miss the point for one simple reason. Healing is part of the character of God.

In the verse above, we read that one of God's names is Yahweh-your-healer (*Yahweh-rophe*). When God reveals his name, as we have seen, we need to take notice, because it is a revelation of his character. Healing is not something God did once and may or may not do now. It is part of who he is.

Look at Exodus 15 in the story of Israel. The people of God have escaped Egypt, but now are about to die of thirst in the wilderness, so they are grumbling. It doesn't take much. In the last few days they have witnessed nine plagues and been delivered from all of them; been spared from the angel of death while the Egyptian firstborn all died; been led by the cloud and the pillar of fire to the Red Sea; and seen the sea miraculously parted and then miraculously closed again over the Egyptians. Yet here they are, grumbling because they do not have safe drinking water. Once again, they need the power of God, but this time, it is his healing power. So God uses the event to reveal a new name to them.

You see, at this point the Israelites did not see God as a healer.

They knew he could kill, because he had killed and afflicted countless Egyptians during the plagues and exodus. But they needed to know that at the root, in his very nature, he was not a killer or an afflicter, but a healer. They needed to know that killing and afflicting were things he sometimes did to protect his people, but that in his character, he had always been a healing God, a God who rescued and brought life and made whole. They needed to know him as Yahweh-your-healer.

We do too. It's tragic when you hear people doubt that God heals today, because the Bible clearly teaches that healing is part of his character, and that he never changes. It also gives overwhelming evidence of healings, signs, and wonders taking place through (at least) Jesus, the twelve, the seventy-two, Stephen, Philip, Ananias, Paul, Barnabas, and the Corinthian and Galatian churches—and it gives no indication that this is something that was only meant to be around for a few years.[1] So it should not surprise us when God heals people today, and in the same sorts of ways as he did in Scripture: fixing limbs and restoring sight, giving hearing to the deaf and babies to the barren woman, healing people from deadly poison, casting out demons, and even raising people from the dead. He is, after all, Yahweh-your-healer.

But here's where the rubber hits the road: He actually does those things. Not just in theory, but in practice. In fact, even in the course of writing this book, I have witnessed all of the types of healings I just listed, either by seeing them happen in front of me or talking to the particular individual afterward.[2] This is not because I, or my church, are particularly good or obedient people. It is certainly not because we are more good or obedient than the person down the road who hasn't been healed. It is simply because we believe in and worship Yahweh-your-healer.

Healing is not just something God did for a certain period in history and then stopped. It is part of his name; it is who he is. Yahweh-your-healer was his name when the Israelites came out of Egypt, and still is today. And it always will be.

Endnotes

1. For these examples of healing, see Matthew 10:1; Mark 1:30-31; Luke 10:9, 17-19; John 5:1-9; Acts 6:8; 8:7; 9:17; 14:3, 9-10; 19:11-12; 28:3-6; 1 Corinthians 12:9, 28; Galatians 3:5. Excellent scriptural arguments for the supernatural gifts continuing today can be found in, for instance, D. A. Carson, Showing the Spirit *(Grand Rapids, MI: Baker, 1987); Wayne Grudem,* Systematic Theology *(Grand Rapids, MI: Zondervan, 1994), chapters 17 and 52; Jack Deere,* Surprised by the Power of the Spirit *(Grand Rapids, MI: Zondervan, 1993). Each of these books mentions specific contemporary examples.*

2. For those readers who might think this sounds like a televangelist who has taken leave of his or her senses, I recommend Jack Deere's Surprised by the Power of the Spirit, *www. kingschurch.eu/evidence, and Mark 16:15–20.*

STOP AND STUDY

The fact that God heals is obvious from Scripture, but you may never have experienced or witnessed God's healing power, so you may have trouble believing in it. There are two solutions to this. The first, which is by far the most important, is to go through Scripture carefully and study the healing power of God (the Bible is full of examples, but some good places to start are 2 Kings 4—5; Luke 7—8; and Acts 9). The second, which will supplement this but not replace it, is to read stories of God healing people around the world.

The following resources may help you. You won't agree with everything in all of them—neither does this author!—but they should increase your faith in Yahweh-your-healer.

Jack Deere, *Surprised by the Power of the Spirit* (Grand Rapids, MI: Zondervan, 1993).

—A full length biblical argument for the existence of spiritual gifts today, together with lots of evidence of modern healings, from a former cessationist. If you struggle with the idea that God might do New Testament style miracles today, this will help you.

Wayne Grudem, *Systematic Theology* (Grand Rapids, MI: Zondervan, 1994); see the chapters on "Miracles" (355–372) and "Gifts of the Holy Spirit" (1016–1088).

—Grudem's magnificent review of theology includes three chapters that talk about spiritual gifts, including healing, continuing today. The chapters are rooted in Scripture, but include some contemporary examples.

D. A. Carson, *Showing the Spirit* (Grand Rapids, MI: Baker, 1987).

—This theological exposition of 1 Corinthians 12—14 is careful, balanced, and biblical, and looks at how Paul understood the use of spiritual gifts in the church.

John Wimber, *Power Healing* (San Francisco: Harper & Row, 1987; London: Hodder and Stoughton, 1986).

—The founder of the Vineyard churches explains his theology of healing and gives numerous examples of it in action.

Phil Moore, "A Healthy Theology of Healing," available free at www.kingschurch.eu/library.

—A short paper on the various theological approaches to healing, with practical implications.

Brother Yun and Paul Hattaway, *The Heavenly Man* (Oxford: Monarch, 2002).

—You will feel like you are back in the book of Acts, complete with all sorts of healings and miracles, in this powerful story of Chinese Christian Brother Yun.

Questions for personal application

1. Do you believe that God is still able and willing to heal people today?

2. Read through James 5:13–18. What instructions does James give on how to pray for healing? How could you, and your church, increase your effectiveness in praying to Yahweh-your-healer?

YAHWEH-MY-BANNER

• • • • • •

And Moses built an altar and called the name of it, Yahweh-
my-banner, saying, "A hand upon the throne of Yahweh! Yahweh
will have war with Amalek from generation to generation."
—*Exodus 17:15–16*

Sometimes the Bible can be very confusing. We live thousands of miles and thousands of years away from all of it, separated from the people who wrote it by geography, language, culture, history, and (often) even religion. So it can frequently be baffling. There you are, casually reading through Paul's letter to a friend, and suddenly he's announcing that "Cretans are always liars, evil beasts, lazy gluttons" (Titus 1:12). Or one minute you're reading a normal love story, the next minute people are exchanging sandals (Ruth 4:7). Understanding the Bible takes effort sometimes, to bridge the gap between the writers and us.

This is also true in Exodus 17. Israel defeats Amalek because

Moses holds the staff of God high in the air, and to celebrate, Moses builds an altar and calls it "Yahweh-my-banner" (*Yahweh-nissi*). When I first read that, I couldn't work it out: Banners are things you wave at football games and hang at parties, so what on earth is one doing here? I later learned that a banner in those days was not the same as it is today. When we understand what it was, the whole story—and the revelation of God's next compound name—make perfect sense.

A banner (the Hebrew word *nes*) was a pole or a flagstaff, the king's standard which would be taken into battle, and it had two purposes. First, it acted as a symbol for the army, a sign of which side you were fighting on (as it does in Jeremiah 51:12). This idea continued well into modern times, and even today people play Capture the Flag at camps or when they go paint-balling. The army's strength and security is bound up with the strength and security of their banner—if it is vulnerable, they will lose, but if it is impregnable, they will win. You may know that, in chess, it doesn't matter how few pieces you have on the board, you can't lose unless your king is captured. In other words, your strength doesn't matter if you have a strong banner.

Secondly, a banner would often serve as a rallying point (as it does in Isaiah 11:10–12). This sounds a bit alien to us in our world of tanks and radios but remember that, in those days, combat was hand-to-hand. You would be fighting one person at a time, and by the time you had defeated him, you could be miles away from the center of the action, so you needed a rallying point, somewhere you could know you were safe, and where you could be given new orders. When Psalm 60:4 says, "You have set up a banner for those who fear you, that they may flee to it from the bow," it is talking about a place to find safety during battle. So the banner was the place you would go to when you needed direction or safety.

Can you see now why Moses calls the altar Yahweh-my-banner? Yahweh is both of these things to his people. He is their standard, their security, and their ensign, and their strength in the fight doesn't really matter if they have a strong banner. He is also their rallying point, the one to whom they run for safety and new instructions during the battle. My approach in life tends to be to get myself into trouble, and then shout, "Banner come here, I'm in trouble, Yahweh come here!" The right approach, however, is to look up from my trouble, locate the position of Yahweh-my-banner, and flee to him for safety and direction.

There is another reason, though, for the revelation of God's name as Yahweh-my-banner in this passage. The point of the story in Exodus 17 is that the efforts of the soldiers on the battlefield were irrelevant: The only thing that mattered was whether the banner was lifted high or not. On paper, Israel had no chance of defeating Amalek. But when their banner was lifted high, they prevailed because Yahweh was infinitely more powerful than either side. God wanted to teach his people that their success or failure did not result from their military strength, but from their dependence on him. (By the way, this is a lesson that Joshua learned. His victories were achieved by absolute dependence on God—not many wars are won by wandering round in circles blowing trumpets—and no Jewish historian ever gives him credit for winning even one battle. He is not even mentioned among the heroes of faith in Hebrews 11, because his victories were all attributed to Yahweh.)

We need to learn this. No matter how strong or weak we are, our success or failure depends on Yahweh. When you are up against it, realize that fighting harder in your own strength is not the answer. Call out to, flee toward, and find safety in Yahweh-my-banner.

YAHWEH-WHO-SANCTIFIES-YOU

• • • • • •

Consecrate yourselves, therefore, and be holy, for I am Yahweh your
God. Keep my statutes and do them; I am Yahweh-who-sanctifies-you.
—Leviticus 20:7–8

Have you ever tried reading Leviticus? It's hard work. Genesis tells
you about Adam and Eve, Abraham and Isaac, Jacob and Joseph, then
Exodus tells you about plagues and a dramatic escape, but Leviticus
is just laws and rituals. You get musicals like *Joseph and the Amazing*
Technicolor Dreamcoat and films like *The Prince of Egypt,* but I doubt if
Fifty Steps to Cleansing Yourself from Skin Diseases would be as popular.
Why is it telling me about how to smear blood on the altar? Why
should I care how to cleanse my house from mildew? So after a couple
of chapters of Leviticus, most people give up.

Now I would give a few tips to anyone trying to read Leviticus
for the first time. First, when you are reading about sacrifices, rejoice

115

in the fact that we no longer need to go through all that, because Jesus has offered a perfect sacrifice, once and for all (Heb. 10:10–14). Second, realize how totally committed God is to having a people who are set apart for him. Think about how pure the Israelites had to be, and how different from the nations around them. Third, consider how clearly the book makes the connection between sin and death—the Israelites had to kill the sacrificial animals themselves (Lev. 1:5), so that they could see the consequences of their sin. Reflect on how much sin matters.

Last, keep coming back to Leviticus 20:8. Without it, the series of commands to be holy can seem not just repetitive, but deeply depressing, leading to all sorts of scary questions. How can we possibly be holy? How can we ever be pure enough to stand before God? And so on and so on. But with it, we have an answer to these questions through one of God's names: "I am Yahweh-who-sanctifies-you" (*Yahweh-m'qadesh*). To sanctify simply means to make holy, so the name "Yahweh-who-sanctifies-you" means "Yahweh who makes you holy." In other words, our holiness does not depend on us, but on God.

This is extraordinary. Even in the old covenant, even in the midst of all these rules, regulations, and rituals that explain what man must do for holiness, it is still acknowledged that it is Yahweh, ultimately, who makes us holy. Remember, the Israelites didn't know about the cross. They didn't believe that the Spirit lives in every believer, either. Yet it was revealed to them that Yahweh was the one who made them holy, and that this was his name, an unchanging feature of his character. No matter where you live in history, you are only made holy by God.

How does this work? How can something so alien to us become possible? Well, think about something you're naturally awful at. For me, it's DIY projects. Recently, I have managed to cut off all the water in my flat, blow the power of a building, and electrocute myself off the main supply. So if someone said to me that he was going to make me a DIY expert, I would laugh at him. How would he achieve it? Giving me a guidebook would help, if I read it, but I have used them in the past and still made a mess of things. Practice would also help, but I'd never get there with that alone, and I'd get everything wrong in the meantime. The only way it would happen would be if a complete DIY expert came to live with me, and showed me how to do every little thing, one step at a time, throughout my life. That would eventually make me an expert at DIY.

This is the way God makes us holy. He gives us a book, which helps, if we read it. He encourages us to practice. But far more than this, he gives us a complete holiness expert—the *Holy* Spirit—to come and live in us, to show us how to do every little thing, one step at a time. And through this process, he makes us holy.

The best illustration of this I have ever heard is from Judson Cornwall.[1] He describes a large ship coming into a river estuary, wanting to get up river to a port. Rivers can be very difficult to navigate, and the ship's captain doesn't know the river well enough to make it on his own, so he radios for a harbor-pilot. The harbor-pilot is someone who knows the river like the back of his hand, and can point out all the pitfalls and dangers the ship might face. As he arrives on board, the captain says, "Thank you for coming, sir. Now, if you could just take the wheel, we'll be on our way." But the harbor-pilot replies, "No sir, that is not an option. I am not licensed to take over. I can tell you what I think you should do, but you have to make the decisions." So as the captain steers the ship, the harbor-pilot makes suggestions that the captain can follow: "Twenty degrees starboard here, sir." "Slow down for this section." "Take this bend wider, sir." And so on. It is up to the captain to make the decisions and take the advice of the harbor-pilot. However, occasionally, the captain might ignore the harbor-pilot, do things his own way, and potentially crash the ship.

When we repent, we admit that we don't know how to live a holy life, so we ask God for help, and he gives us the Holy Spirit to come and live in us. It can be tempting to say, "Oh Holy Spirit, thank you for coming. Now if you'd just take over my life, I'll be on my way." But he replies, "No, that is not an option. Jesus died on the cross so you could get your free will back, and I am not allowed to take it away again. You have to make the decisions." So as we live our lives, he gives us suggestions that we can follow: Stop hanging around with that crowd. Give more this month. Get up half an hour earlier to spend time with me. And so on.

Isn't this astonishing? Even more astonishingly, the Holy Spirit did not live in people like this when Leviticus was written, yet God still revealed himself to Moses as Yahweh-who-sanctifies-you. But this is because, as with his other names, making people holy is not just something God does. It is who he is.

Endnote
1. Judson Cornwall, speaking on God's Excellent Name *at Malvern in 1988.*

YAHWEH-IS-PEACE

• • • • • •

And Gideon said, "Alas, O Lord Yahweh! For now I have seen the
angel of Yahweh face to face." But Yahweh said to him, "Peace
be to you. Do not fear; you shall not die." Then Gideon built
an altar there to Yahweh and called it Yahweh-is-peace.
—Judges 6:22–24

Peace is popular. You very rarely come across those who don't think
peace is a good idea, and if you do, the chances are that other people
don't like them very much. Organizations, charities, pop-culture
movements, even revolutions, have been established because people
desire peace. No one ever came back from a conference, smiling at the
newspaper reporters, proudly announcing they had achieved "war in
our time." Peace is perhaps the most sought-after thing in the world
today. Yet the people seeking it are not finding it. In fact, the people
seeking it often don't know what it is.

Peace is thought of by many people as simply the absence of fighting. War and peace are opposites, they think, so if you don't have war,
you have peace. But this is not the case. You can be filled with incredible peace in the midst of turmoil, and you can be thousands of miles
from war, yet without any peace at all. Most people you know are
probably like this. This is because peace is not just the absence of war,
but something much more positive. The Hebrew word *shalom*, which
means peace, is about wholeness, completeness, welfare, and fullness,
and it is possible even when there is trouble on every side.

A competition was set up during World War II, offering a prize
for the painting that best illustrated peace. Lots of paintings came in
of pastoral scenes, quiet countrysides, and so on, but there was one
that was completely unlike the others. It was of a raging waterfall in
a storm: blackened clouds, torrential rain, and water crashing everywhere. Out of the center of the waterfall came a branch, and on the
branch was a bird, in full-throated song. It won first prize.[1]

When God reveals himself as *Yahweh-shalom*, or "Yahweh-is-
peace," this is what he means. There is no guarantee that there will
never be fighting if we are with God. In fact, we know that there *will*
be fighting, and we know from Scripture that "Yahweh is a man of
war" (Ex. 15:3). The guarantee is that even when there is conflict on
every side, Yahweh will be our *shalom*: our peace, our fullness, our
wholeness, our completeness.

This is Gideon's experience in Judges 6. Israel is under constant attack
from the Midianites, who keep roving around the country ruining their
crops. Gideon is so scared, he is doing something ridiculous. He is threshing his wheat *in a winepress* to keep it out of their sight. Threshing wheat

requires the wind, to separate the wheat from the chaff. How much threshing do you think he can get done in a hole in the ground? The answer is, of
course, not much! Gideon is only down there because he is terrified. And
into this setting, the angel of Yahweh comes and makes it worse: He tells
Gideon that God is going to save Israel out of Midian's hand.

On paper, this is as unpeaceful a situation as you could imagine:
war, fear, and danger. Yet it is in this situation that Yahweh chooses to
reveal a fifth compound name, Yahweh-is-peace. God does not promise him that war will stop. Quite the opposite: He tells him war will
continue, that Gideon has to lead it, and that he has to take on the
most powerful army in the world with only three hundred men! But
in the midst of this chaotic and frightening situation, Yahweh brings
Gideon strength, and wholeness, and fullness, and courage. So Gideon
builds an altar there, and calls it "Yahweh-is-peace." When the battle
is eventually fought, of course, he wins.

Have you noticed that God does not remove us from trouble and
battle? Rather, he gives us all the peace we need to overcome it. He could
remove war, but instead he helps us fight it, with "the readiness given
by the gospel of *peace*" (Eph. 6:15). He could have made us noncomba-
tants, but instead he made us "more than conquerors through him who
loved us" (Rom. 8:37). He could have removed evil from the world, but
instead he made "the *peace* of God, which surpasses all understanding"
the sentry that patrols our hearts and minds (Phil. 4:7).

Peace can be in our centers, even in the heart of the spiritual battle.
And it all comes from Yahweh-is-peace.

Endnote
1. *Judson Cornwall, speaking on* God's Excellent Name *at Malvern in 1988.*

PAUSE AND PRAY

It is important to turn theology into prayer, and this is never more true than with the fact that God is our peace. We can know it in our minds, but our prayers show whether we really believe it. It may be worth praying the following out loud, particularly if you struggle with anxiety and fear.

> *Father, you are Yahweh-is-peace. In you alone there is freedom from fear, shelter from the storm, and fullness of life. Thank you that, for thousands of years, you have been sustaining people who call on your name, and you have never once been threatened, or wrong-footed, or confused. You are all I need.*

> *Jesus, Prince of Peace, I am sorry for my fears, and I ask for your forgiveness. I acknowledge that you are able to provide for me and to sustain me. You clothe the grass and feed the birds, so I can be absolutely certain you will look after me. Not only that, but you have promised never to leave me or forsake me, and you have never broken your word. So*

I choose to believe that you are in control of every situation, and I thank you for being my peace.

And now, Lord, I ask for the peace of God, which passes all understanding, to guard my heart and mind in Christ Jesus. I believe that in you is wholeness, completion, freedom from anxiety, and life in abundance, and I ask you now to fill me with your Holy Spirit so I can know and experience your everlasting peace. Amen.

YAHWEH-MY-SHEPHERD

• • • • • •

*Yahweh-my-shepherd; I shall not want. He makes me lie down
in green pastures. He leads me beside still waters. He restores my
soul. He leads me in paths of righteousness for his name's sake.*
—Psalm 23:1–3

Did you know that the word *sheep* appears in the Bible more than the
word *grace*, over twice as often as the word *pray*, and nearly three times
more than the word *church*? Or that the New Testament uses *shepherd*
seven times as often as *Christian*? Shepherds (and sheep) were everywhere
in the ancient world, and everyone knew about them. In our industrial-
ized world, though, most people have never met one. So when we hear
God called a shepherd, we don't really understand what is being said.

We need to. God is described as a shepherd numerous times in
Scripture, and in the most famous psalm of them all, quoted above, we
see that one of his names is *Yahweh-rohi*, or "Yahweh-my-shepherd."

124

So it is worth having a look at a few of the things shepherds did, and how the picture applies to God.

First, shepherding was a humble and unglamorous job. Sheep stink! No one wanted to be around them—being a shepherd was dirty, demeaning, dangerous, and dull, what with having only animals for company. It involved sleeping outside, fighting off wild animals, and being generally looked down upon by everyone else, which is why David, the youngest brother, was given the job. Yet God was prepared to be known as a shepherd, from Genesis onward. Yahweh was prepared to get in among dirty, smelly, difficult, stubborn people, in order to care for them.

Second, shepherds provided for their sheep. Sheep were not responsible for finding lush pastures; the shepherd was. If there was no water, that was the shepherd's responsibility. The shepherd provided for every one of the sheep's needs, because he knew how to sort out things like food and water, and the sheep didn't. As we have seen, Yahweh is a provider by nature, so this aspect of the picture is easy to understand. David makes it clear that this is what he has in mind when he says, "Yahweh is my shepherd; I shall not want." Having God as your shepherd means you lack nothing you need.

Third, shepherds protected their flock. Wild animals like lions, bears, and wolves, as well as human thieves, threatened sheep, and the shepherd's job was to keep them safe. This would sometimes involve him putting his own life at risk for their sake, through fighting the intruder; it would always involve him keeping the flock together, since a sheep that had wandered off on its own would be in great danger (see Luke 15:1–7, for instance). God does the same. He fights off evil, even when we walk through the valley of the shadow of death, and he keeps us together, protecting us from ourselves as well as from others. These two ways of protecting—through defense and discipline—are summarized by David as "your rod," a wooden cudgel used to fight enemies and protect the sheep, and "your staff," used to round up the flock. It is worth pointing out that human shepherds, called "pastors" or "elders" in the Bible, have the same two responsibilities (Acts 20:25–31).

Fourth, shepherds led their sheep. It was not up to the sheep to find their way; it was up to the shepherd to lead them there. On their own, sheep might go toward turbulent rivers and fall in, or wander from the right path into danger. The shepherd, however, would lead them by still waters and in the right (or righteous) paths, taking full responsibility for them being where he wanted them to be. You would never see a sheep debating with the shepherd about where it was supposed to be going, or wondering whether the shepherd's will for it had changed. When the shepherd moved on, so would the sheep. So assuming a sheep was not disobedient, it would always be safe.

Lots of people get very worried about whether or not they are walking in the will of God. If you are, you need to realize how much bigger "Yahweh-my-shepherd" is than you. He has seen every possible pitfall in your life, he is leading you in paths of righteousness for his name's sake, and eventually you will dwell in the house of Yahweh forever. You cannot do what he says and still end up in the wrong place. So unless you have been disobedient to him, you are exactly where he wants you to be!

When we get worried about God's will for our lives, we need to remember: We are just sheep. And Yahweh is our shepherd.

YAHWEH-OUR-RIGHTEOUSNESS

· · · · · ·

Behold, the days are coming, declares Yahweh, when I will raise up
for David a righteous Branch, and he shall reign as king and deal
wisely, and shall execute justice and righteousness in the land. In his
days Judah will be saved, and Israel will dwell securely. And this is
the name by which he will be called: Yahweh-our-righteousness.
—Jeremiah 23:5–6

A Greek proverb says, "The fish stinks from the head down." This is such
a good metaphor for leadership. Look all around you, and if you see a
floundering family, country, company, or church, the odds are that it will
start with the leadership. If a soccer team is letting in too many goals, they
don't fire the goalkeeper; they fire the manager. At the other extreme, if
a company doubles its profits, it's the CEO who gets a massive bonus.
Both these types of situation often seem unfair, but they happen because,
somehow, organizations take on the characteristics of their leaders.

It is the same in the Old Testament. If you read Kings and Chronicles, you will find that Israel and Judah rise and fall according to the behavior of their kings. Because God puts authority in place, you will find that evil kings produce an evil country (under Ahab, in 1 Kings 16—19, there were only seven thousand believing Jews left), but that good kings can bring about spiritual revival (like the one under Josiah in 2 Chronicles 34—35). So God takes leadership extremely seriously.

This is why God is so angry with bad leaders—both the royal house and the prophets—in Jeremiah 23. He delegated responsibility to them—the vital task of shepherding his people, looking after them, and protecting them—yet instead of doing this, the leaders destroyed and scattered the people, and led them astray. There was a famous case in the Vietnam War, when a squadron of soldiers, led by Lieutenant William Calley, massacred a Vietnamese village. The sense of outrage in the military, and the punishment of Lieutenant Calley, was quite right: The generals had given him the job of looking after his men, and he had corrupted them and caused them to commit atrocities. This gives a sense of what Yahweh feels in this chapter.

To overcome the problem of bad leadership, which had plagued Israel from the beginning, Yahweh promises that he is going to raise up a righteous king, one who will bring about "justice and righteousness in the land" (23:5). So far, so good. But he then gives him a very surprising name.

If you have read through Jeremiah 23 until this point, you would expect the king's name to be something like "Yahweh is righteous." That's the contrast, isn't it? The shepherds are unrighteous and cause injustice, but the coming king will be righteous and bring justice. But that is not what God says. Instead, the king is given the name *Yahweh-tsidkenu*, or "Yahweh-our-righteousness." Do you see the difference? It is not just that the king is going to be righteous; he is, but that is not the point. The point is, he is going to be righteous *on behalf of his people*. He is going to be *their*—in fact, *our*—righteousness.

Perhaps another military picture will help make this clear. The film *Troy* starts with a battle lineup between two massive armies. The rival kings negotiate and agree that, to save lives, one man from each side should be chosen to fight on behalf of his army. Whichever man wins, his army will have the other as their slaves. Achilles is chosen by the Greeks to go and fight for them, and even though he is much smaller than the man he is fighting, he kills him immediately. (By the way, did you notice that this is almost identical to the story of David and Goliath?) As a result, the entire Greek army wins, and takes their opponents as slaves. None of them has so much as lifted a sword, but they get all the rights and privileges of victory, because of what Achilles achieved.

This illustrates what is meant by the name Yahweh-our-righteousness. Yahweh is promising a day when Israel will not just have a king who is righteous, but a king who is righteous on behalf of his people. He is promising that generations of Lieutenant Calleys will be replaced by an Achilles, a champion, a leader whose righteousness will be given freely to his people. Living this side of Calvary, we know that this is "Christ Jesus, who became to us wisdom from God, righteousness and sanctification and redemption, so that, as it is written, 'Let the one who boasts, boast in the Lord'" (1 Cor. 1:30–31).

Our righteousness does not come from ourselves, any more than the Greeks won the battle because they were skillful fighters. No, our righteousness—and, therefore, our boasting—rests entirely in our "righteous branch." In our champion, King Jesus. In Yahweh-our-righteousness.

YAHWEH-IS-THERE

· · · · · ·

And the name of the city from that time on will be: "Yahweh-is-there."
—*Ezekiel 48:35*

Here's another riddle for you. Imagine you are in a room, and everyone else leaves. How many people are there in the room?

The way you answer that question says a lot about you. Most people would say one. Atheists would also say one (unless they are first-year philosophy students, in which case they might say none). Agnostics would say one. Lots of religious people would as well: Buddhists, for instance, or many Muslims, who do not believe that Allah is very imminent. New Agers might believe there was something else there, but they wouldn't describe it as a person. So all of these people, when, for example, driving a car or staying in a hotel on a business trip, would feel they were completely alone.

When Ezekiel starts prophesying, the Jews are the same. They know they worship a transcendent God—that is, a God who is enthroned above all, untouchably huge and sovereign and other than them—but they also know he lives in a very specific place. They would tell you: "Man used to walk with God, but in the garden of Eden we lost this privilege, and God now lives in a box, a four-foot-by-two-foot-by-two-foot box. That box (the ark of the covenant) used to be kept in a tent (the tabernacle), and it is now in a building (the Temple). And worst of all, we are stuck in exile in Babylon, and the Temple is in Jerusalem, hundreds of miles away from us, so we can't worship him or be near him. God is still transcendent, but he isn't very imminent. He isn't very there."

God knows that this is the way they see things, so he sends them a prophet. And although the book of Ezekiel can be difficult to read in places, two things come through very clearly. First, God is still very much transcendent, as we will see in another reflection. But second, God is imminent, he is there, he is with his people where they are. Ezekiel 1 starts with a revelation of God, not in the Temple, but by a Babylonian canal, which would have seemed to be a very strange idea to a Jew in exile. In chapter 10, there is a quite shocking vision of the glory of Yahweh leaving the Temple altogether, and standing by the east gate, facing Babylon. Ezekiel is saying to the exiles that God is not bound by a geographic location, but that he is wherever they are. They are not alone.

A few years later, the Temple is destroyed altogether by the Babylonians, and Ezekiel ends his book by prophesying about a new temple. People get very excited about what the details of this vision might mean, but don't get worried about that—it is basically using apocalyptic language to describe the new temple: the people of God. (Incidentally, this is something that the New Testament writers pick up on and develop).[1] The book finishes in the most dramatic way possible, like a soap opera ending with a cliff-hanger, with the revelation of God's final compound name: *Yahweh-shammah*, or "Yahweh-is-there."

The odds are that, of all the compound names of Yahweh we have looked at, this would have been the most astonishing to the Jews. Not only was Yahweh saying he was not bound to stay in the Temple, but he also was saying that he would be wherever his people were, even if that was in pagan, sick, evil Babylon. His very name, Yahweh-is-there, meant that he would never abandon them, that they could never be alone, and that they could always worship him. No matter how far they strayed or how sinful they had been, God's faithfulness to his own name meant that he would always be there.

I am writing this reflection in the middle of nowhere, high in the French mountains. I am on my own in the house, and I had to walk the last bit of my journey here, because my car couldn't make it uphill through the thick snow. There is a hill less than a mile away that I cannot even see because of the snow and the clouds, and there is a fair possibility I may get trapped here. Physically, I am as isolated as you can be; even the people whom I can reach from here don't speak my language. But as a result of who my God is, I am not alone. Far from it. Yahweh is here.

And if you are a disciple of Jesus, no matter what your situation is, he is where you are too.

So back to our riddle: What's the smallest number of people—or perhaps I should say persons—who can ever be in a room where you are? Four. The Father who gave up his only Son for you, the Son who is praying for you, the Spirit who was hovering over the face of the deep when the world was created and now lives in you, and you. Sometimes circumstances may be really tough, and it may not feel like that. But it is still true. Wherever you are, whatever you're doing, he is Yahweh-is-there.

Endnote

1. See, for a start, 1 Corinthians 3:16–17; 2 Corinthians 6:16; Ephesians 2:21. Revelation 21—22 expands the vision of Ezekiel, using similar imagery, but with the city representing the people of God, and the Temple representing God himself.

WAIT AND WORSHIP

Unlike anyone else in the world, Christians worship a God who is there, a person and friend who is near at all times. This hymn reflects on the nearness of God, and was written by John Bode in 1868.

O Jesus, I have promised to serve Thee to the end;
Be Thou forever near me, my Master and my Friend;
I shall not fear the battle if Thou art by my side,
Nor wander from the pathway if Thou wilt be my Guide.

O let me feel Thee near me! The world is ever near;
I see the sights that dazzle, the tempting sounds I hear;
My foes are ever near me, around me and within;
But Jesus, draw me near Thou, and shield my soul from sin.

O let me hear Thee speaking in accents clear and still,
Above the storms of passion, the murmurs of self will.
O speak to reassure me, to hasten or control;
O speak, and make me listen, Thou Guardian of my soul.

O Jesus, Thou hast promised to all who follow Thee
That where Thou art in glory there shall Thy servant be.

And Jesus, I have promised to serve Thee to the end;
O give me grace to follow, my Master and my Friend.

O let me see Thy footprints, and in them plant mine own;
My hope to follow duly is in Thy strength alone.
O guide me, call me, draw me, uphold me to the end;
And then in Heaven receive me, my Savior and my Friend.

A wonderful contemporary song about the God who is there, which I frequently use in my devotions, is "Everything" by Tim Hughes, © 2007 Survivor Records, which is based on an ancient prayer.

God in my living, there in my breathing
God in my waking, God in my sleeping
God in my resting, there in my working
God in my thinking, God in my speaking

Be my everything

God in my hoping, there in my dreaming
God in my watching, God in my waiting
God in my laughing, there in my weeping
God in my hurting, God in my healing

Christ in me, Christ in me, Christ in me, the hope of glory
You are everything

Christ in me, Christ in me, Christ in me, the hope of glory

Be my everything

Be my everything

THE MOST HIGH

• • • • • •

At the end of the days I, Nebuchadnezzar, lifted my eyes to heaven,
and my reason returned to me, and I blessed the Most High, and praised
and honored him who lives forever, for his dominion is an everlasting
dominion, and his kingdom endures from generation to generation; all the
inhabitants of the earth are accounted as nothing, and he does according
to his will among the host of heaven and among the inhabitants of the
earth; and none can stay his hand or say to him, "What have you done?"
—Daniel 4:34–35

"Power tends to corrupt; absolute power corrupts absolutely."[1] No
matter where you look in human history, you can find examples:
pharaohs and caesars, popes and kings. This is why countries
today spread power between heads of state, elected officials, the law
courts, the media, and everyone else. Democracy reduces the amount
of power any one person has, and so usually leads to less abuse. This

is called the separation of powers, and it is foundational to many modern governments.

The funny thing is, separation of powers is not in the Bible. That doesn't mean we shouldn't do it—driving cars is not in the Bible either. But it can skew our thinking. Some churches act like parliaments, making decisions by what the people think rather than what God thinks. Some theology faculties act like a Supreme Court, sitting and passing judgment on whether what God said was true or not. Some Christians act like the media, forever talking about what God says rather than doing anything about it. In subtle ways, we often set ourselves up as authorities who can somehow keep God accountable.

But this is why we need the Bible. Scripture has such a big, sweeping, glorious vision of Yahweh that our patronizing and God-shrinking logic evaporates before it. In the verses above, a ruthless pagan king called Nebuchadnezzar realizes how great God's dominion actually is. He knows what he's talking about—he used to be the most powerful man in the world himself, referred to as the "king of kings," before he was reduced to a hairy, long-nailed, grass-eating madman for his arrogance (Dan. 4:29–33). Yet faced with the vastness and wonder of Almighty God, Nebuchadnezzar is broken.

He starts by calling God "the Most High," which is remarkable in itself for a pagan king. There were dozens of gods floating around Babylon in the sixth century BC, but Nebuchadnezzar has been shown time and again that there is one God, the Most High, over all things. He has been told what his dream was and what it meant (Dan. 2). He has seen Shadrach, Meshach, and Abednego's sheer zeal in refusing to bow down to his statue, and has then tried to burn them in a furnace only to see them walking around unharmed, with "a son of the gods" walking among them (Dan. 3). He has then had another dream interpreted, and seen it come true (Dan. 4). So his view of God, rightly, is of an all-powerful sovereign, the Most High.

Then he goes further. God is not just the biggest of the gods, but the one who has everlasting dominion over everything. The people of earth are "accounted as nothing," which means that they cannot sway his decisions or block his purposes, and so he does whatever he wills on the earth. In other words, he has complete power. The Most High is not a prime minister of a democratic country. He is an absolute monarch, with total authority to do whatever he likes, wherever and whenever he likes.

Yet he goes further still. Not only is it impossible to stop him, but it is also impossible to question his decisions: "None can stay his hand or say to him, 'What have you done?'" Unlike our politicians, the Most High is not accountable to us. He never needs to give interviews in the Sunday papers to explain himself, or write a manifesto to convince people that he's right. His knowledge and power are both so much greater than ours that anything like that would be faintly ridiculous: the equivalent, as Paul puts it in Romans 9, of a pot saying to the potter, "Why have you made me like this?"

Adjusting to this is hard, but it is necessary. In democratic countries, we can feel that we have a right to put our leaders on trial (which in human terms is not a bad thing), and then we impose this on God. But whereas politicians are humans like us, the Most High is totally beyond us, completely all-powerful, unstoppable, and unaccountable. Even totalitarian rulers—like Louis XIV, Hitler, and of course

Nebuchadnezzar—are held to account eventually, but God is not. It is just as well. Would you volunteer to judge the living God?

"None can stay his hand, or say to him 'What have you done?'" So if we try and hold him accountable, we should not be surprised if our arrogance is shown up for what it is. He is, after all, the Most High.

Endnote
1. This phrase was first coined by the British historian Lord Acton in a letter to Bishop Mandell Creighton in 1887.

YAHWEH OF HOSTS

• • • • • •

O Yahweh of hosts, God of Israel, enthroned above the
cherubim, you are the God, you alone, of all the king-
doms of the earth; you have made heaven and earth.
—Isaiah 37:16

If you want to know how powerful someone is, look at his army. Dictators know this, which is why, as soon as they get control, they organize
a huge military rally to show off how strong they are. Democracies
know it, which is why they have such huge defense budgets. Cinema-
goers know it, which is why when you watch an epic film, and see a
massive army marching for as far as the eye can see, you know that
the most powerful leader in the film is joining battle. Even kids know
it: "My dad's stronger than your dad" is another way of saying "The
force that I can call upon is greater than yours." If you ever see a truly
powerful leader, the size of their army will bear witness to this.

This is one reason why God is referred to in Scripture as "Yahweh of hosts." It's a funny phrase that we don't really use today, but it is a name that refers to God's command of "the heavenly hosts," the army of angels that he has at his disposal.[1] It is a way of articulating how great God is by showing the size and strength of the army that serves him. So one way of considering the greatness of God is to look at his army.

The foot soldiers of God's army are called angels. Despite centuries of paintings that present angels as chubby children floating around playing harps and trumpets, angels in Scripture look like men, are often dressed in dazzling white, and have frightening power. Do you know what the largest number of people ever killed in one day's fighting was? It was not 52,000 at the Somme, or even 80,000 or thereabouts in Hiroshima; but 185,000, obliterated by the angel of Yahweh in the camp of the Assyrians in Isaiah 37. This event still puzzles secular historians today, but the Bible is very clear: The king of Assyria, rather foolishly, challenged the power of Yahweh to rescue his people. The king of Judah cried for help, as we have just read, and Yahweh responded by sending an angel to wipe out the Assyrians and display his power. Not all the angels, just one of them. Angels are powerful.

As you move through the ranks of angelic beings, however, the thing that strikes you is not their power or majesty, but the power and majesty of the one they work for. Angels spend their time singing "Glory to God in the highest" (Luke 2:14). Mighty angels refuse to accept any praise from man, and channel it to God (Rev. 19:10). The archangel doesn't speak on his own authority, but uses the Lord's instead (Jude 9). Cherubim—particularly powerful angels—are simply God's chariot, his throne (Ps. 18:10). No matter how high up the heavenly hierarchy you get, you never find a single one who tries to draw attention to himself. It would be blasphemous.

In fact, this increases the nearer to God you get. If you look at Isaiah 6, you find truly terrifying creatures called seraphim. They shout, and the Temple shakes: We're not talking boys' choirs and harps, but Harrier jump jets and rockets breaking the sound barrier as they deafen all around them. Yet these astonishingly powerful beings have a pair of wings set aside for the express purpose of covering their eyes, so that they don't actually look straight at God, and they call continually, "Holy, holy, holy is Yahweh of hosts; the whole earth is full of his glory!" How awesome do you have to be, to make sinless, ground-shaking angels cover their eyes so they cannot even see you?

These various creatures, and maybe others, form the heavenly hosts, the armies of heaven at God's command. So in 701 BC, when the king of Judah was confronted by messengers saying, "On what do you rest this trust of yours?" the prophet Isaiah—the same Isaiah who had seen the seraphim, remember—knew what to do. Like the Egyptians and the Philistines before them, the Assyrians were about to discover that picking a fight with Yahweh was a bad idea. All the king of Judah had to do was to cry out to "Yahweh of hosts, God of Israel, who is enthroned above the cherubim," and the invading army was decimated by the morning.

On what do you rest this trust of yours? Make sure it's on Yahweh of hosts.

Endnote
1. *Sometimes the word* hosts *can also refer to human armies, or even the sun, moon, and stars, all of which belong to Yahweh.*

THE ROCK THAT IS HIGHER THAN I

· · · · · ·

Hear my cry, O God, listen to my prayer; from the end of the earth I call to you when my heart is faint. Lead me to the rock that is higher than I, for you have been my refuge, a strong tower against the enemy.
—Psalm 61:1–3

Scotland, December 1862. Storms had shipwrecked a number of boats off the rocky northern coast. Sailors, forced to abandon their ships, had swum through the torrent toward the shore, hoping to reach safety, but had discovered that the cliffs were too steep to climb. Dozens of men, each of them a father or a husband to somebody, had died, battered to death or simply drowned. The young local vicar, hoping to rescue some, began to work tirelessly to chisel steps out of the chalk cliff, so that shipwrecked sailors could climb from the beach to a chamber of safety above it. His efforts saved many lives, with the refuge in the cliffs providing shelter from the storm.

Over time, however, erosion wore away the steps. Within a few winters, sailors who were cast adrift in the area were drowning again, approaching the coastline in hope, only to find that the chamber was too high for them to reach. In many cases, the helpless young men died actually seeing the refuge above them, tantalizingly and excruciatingly out of their grasp. Eventually, it was decided to hang chain ladders from the top of the cliffs, for sailors to climb up to safety.[1]

It is something like this that David has in mind when he talks about "the rock that is higher than I." Today, the picture of God as a rock may suggest all sorts of things to us—solid ground on which to build, unwavering strength, even wonderful views from mountaintops—but in Old Testament Israel, it referred to a place of safety, refuge, and shelter. (In 2 Samuel 22:2–3, David praises Yahweh for being his fortress, deliverer, rock, shield, horn, stronghold, and refuge, and the Psalms generally use these images interchangeably.) A rock was a place where you were safe, both from the weather and from your enemies. The Jewish historian Josephus, describing outlaws hiding from the authorities, gives a good description:

> These rocks were in mountains that were extremely sheer, and around them were nothing but precipices. There were some entrances into the caves, but they were surrounded by sharp rocks, and this is where the brigands lay, hidden, with all their families about them … It was impossible to get up to them, because of the steep sides of the mountains, nor to get down to them from above. (Antiquities, 14:15)

This sort of safety—"surrounded," "hidden," "impossible to get up to"—is what the word "rock" meant to an Old Testament believer. So when David calls Yahweh his rock, he means Yahweh is his place of safety, his salvation.

But the phrase "the rock *that is higher than I*" goes one step further, because it shows that God's deliverance is impossible for David (and us!) to get hold of without receiving it as a gift. Like the sailors spluttering and dying at the foot of the sea cliffs, he knows he cannot help himself, since God's salvation is beyond his reach. The fact that he uses "salvation" to mean military rescue and we use it to mean spiritual rescue does not change anything; in fact, our salvation is even more unattainable by our own efforts than David's was. He had armies, but we have nothing—a floundering, drowning people with no steps and no ladders, just hope in the rock that is higher than us:

Rock of Ages, cleft for me,
Let me hide myself in thee!
Let the water, and the blood
From thy riven side which flowed,
Be for sin the double cure,
Cleanse from wrath, and make me pure.

Nothing in my hand I bring;
Simply to thy cross I cling!
Naked, come to thee for dress,
Helpless, look to thee for grace.
Foul, I to the fountain fly—

Wash me, Savior, or I die!

Nothing in my sinful hands
Can fulfill thy law's demands.
Could my zeal no respite know,
Could my tears forever flow,
All for sin could not atone—
Thou must save, and thou alone!

While I draw this fleeting breath,
When my eyelids close in death,
When I soar through tracts unknown,
See thee on thy judgment throne,
Rock of ages, cleft for me,
Let me hide myself in thee![2]

David's cry was a cry of desperation, rooted in the recognition of his impotence and helplessness, yet also in an acknowledgement of the utter security and strength that is provided by his God. How much more should ours be! "From the end of the earth I call to you when my heart is faint. Lead me to the rock that is higher than I!"

Endnotes
1. *This story is taken from Charles Spurgeon's commentary on this passage.*
2. *The hymn "Rock of Ages," by Augustus Toplady, public domain.*

THE GOD OF ISRAEL

· · · · · ·

And Joshua said to all the people, "Thus says Yahweh, the God of
Israel, 'Long ago, your fathers lived beyond the Euphrates, Terah, the
father of Abraham and of Nahor; and they served other gods.'"
—Joshua 24:2

Yahweh is the God of a people. Two hundred and one times in the Old
Testament he is referred to as the God of Israel, and another thirty-one
times as the Holy One of Israel. Today, in a largely Gentile church and a
largely pagan world, this may seem a little strange, so the name is often
quietly dropped. But we serve an unchanging God. And the apostles, in
seven separate places in the book of Acts, reminded their listeners that they
were proclaiming good news about the God of Israel, the God of their
fathers, the God of Abraham, Isaac, and Jacob. So to know Yahweh, we
need to know him as the God of Israel.

This means understanding three things. First, God chose a people, by grace. We have looked at this elsewhere, but it is made blatant in the verse before us here: Israel is descended from Abraham, and Abraham came from an idol-worshipping family in one of the world's most pagan cities.

Second, God chose a *people*. English-speaking, individualistic Westerners have often missed this idea completely, and ended up with Jesus-and-me Christianity, but Scripture could not be clearer: God wants a people, a community, not a random bunch of individuals all going off in their own directions. In verse 7 of this chapter, he tells the people that they had seen the destruction of the Egyptians, although almost certainly none of those individuals actually had, because he sees the people of Israel as a collective unit. (I do the same every time I claim, "We won the World Cup in 1966." Though I was never on the England team, and wasn't even alive at the time, I use this language to show solidarity with those who were.) Not only that, but throughout the Old Testament, and very directly here, he addresses the nation collectively, not individually. Human beings to God are like blobs of paint to Michelangelo: They only reach their true beauty and potential when combined with others to form his Sistine Chapel, the people of God.

Third, God wants *one* people: the people of Israel. Hang on, you're saying, what about the church? That is a good question, but I believe Scripture clearly teaches us that Israel and the church are not two peoples, but one. Apart from the fact that the word for "church" (*ekklesia*) is used of Israel (Acts 7:38), and the word "Israel" is used of the church (Gal. 6:16), consider for example:

He himself is our peace, who has made us both one ... that he might create in himself one new man in place of the two. (Eph. 2:14–15)

> There is neither Jew nor Greek ... for you are all one in
> Christ Jesus. And if you are Christ's, then you are Abraham's
> offspring, heirs according to promise. (Gal. 3:28–29)

> The Gentiles are fellow heirs, members of the same body,
> and partakers of the promise in Christ Jesus through the
> gospel. (Eph. 3:6)

To illustrate how this works, let's take the image of a river. Near where I live in Eastbourne, UK, there is a river that meanders so widely across the floodplain that it has formed little dead ends of water called oxbow lakes. They contain water, and in some ways are connected to the river, but the real river will ultimately continue on toward the sea without them. Some people see Israel like the river and the church like the oxbow lake. The church is part of God's people, of course, but a slight detour; the main river is the Jewish people, and that is where we should be focusing our attention.

Others imagine Israel to be like a river that stopped flowing completely and got replaced by something else. (There have been examples of this geographical phenomenon in Indonesia, where water has flowed down from the uplands, but the river has then dried up, leaving the rice farmers with nothing to irrigate.) Seen like this, the Jews were once the people of God, but now the people of God have become a new thing. Israel is dead, long live the church! Seen from the perspective of the sea, Israel in this view is a historical oddity, a river which ran for a while but then stopped.

But the Bible presents Israel like the Amazon. In the Peruvian mountains, the Amazon is simply a small trickle of water, which gradually grows in size as it descends. Like the children of the former idol-worshipper from Ur in Babylon, it does not look much to start with, but as time goes on it becomes quite sizeable, and begins to shape the landscape around it. As it reaches the Brazilian rainforest, a whole bunch of other rivers start pouring into it, making it much larger. These tributaries (like the Gentiles) were not part of the original river, but as soon as they flow into it, they take on the same identity as the great body of water now rushing across the drainage basin, and it becomes impossible to separate them from it. In their turn, they make the Amazon far bigger and more spectacular than it ever would have been without them, so that by the time it crashes into the Atlantic, it is carrying more water than the next ten biggest rivers in the world put together, enough to make the salty ocean turn fresh for up to two hundred miles out to sea. "I looked, and behold, a great multitude that no one could number, from every nation, from all tribes and peoples and languages, standing before the throne and before the Lamb" (Rev. 7:9).

Seeing this should help us build local churches that are committed to mission and unity, but it should also show us the God behind the whole thing. As the Sistine Chapel shows the brilliance of Michelangelo and the Amazon declares the praises of its creator, Israel, the church, the people of God—call it what you will—tells us of the consistency and faithfulness and wisdom of Yahweh, the God of Israel.

# READ AND REFLECT

Most people reading this book are probably Gentiles: non-Jews, who have been brought into God's people by an amazing act of grace in Jesus Christ. As we consider the faithfulness of the God of Israel, and the fact that he is now fulfilling his promise to Abraham through people like us, it is good to remember the glorious way he achieved this at the cross.

You might want to meditate on the following truths from Ephesians 2:11–22, giving thanks to God as you read.

> Therefore remember that at one time you Gentiles in the flesh, called "the uncircumcision" by what is called the circumcision, which is made in the flesh by hands— remember that you were at that time separated from Christ, alienated from the commonwealth of Israel and strangers to the covenants of promise, having no hope and without God in the world.
>
> But now in Christ Jesus you who once were far off have been brought near by the blood of Christ. For he himself

is our peace, who has made us both one and has broken down in his flesh the dividing wall of hostility by abolishing the law of commandments expressed in ordinances, that he might create in himself one new man in place of the two, so making peace, and might reconcile us both to God in one body through the cross, thereby killing the hostility.

And he came and preached peace to you who were far off and peace to those who were near. For through him we both have access in one Spirit to the Father.

So then you are no longer strangers and aliens, but you are fellow citizens with the saints and members of the household of God, built on the foundation of the apostles and prophets, Christ Jesus himself being the cornerstone, in whom the whole structure, being joined together, grows into a holy temple in the Lord. In him you also are being built together into a dwelling place for God by the Spirit.

······

EXPLORATION III
God in Three Persons

······

THE TRINITY

• • • • • •

In those days Jesus came from Nazareth of Galilee and was baptized by John in the Jordan. And when he came up out of the water, immediately he saw the heavens being torn open and the Spirit descending on him like a dove. And a voice came from heaven, "You are my beloved Son; with you I am well pleased."
—Mark 1:9–11

The Trinity is thoroughly biblical and thoroughly baffling. For two thousand years it has been the foundation of Christian orthodoxy; denial of the Trinity in some form is a fairly sure sign that a "Christian" group is a cult. At the same time, it is one doctrine that probably no one in church history has fully understood. The pastor and Bible teacher C. J. Mahaney remarked that when you are talking to your children, there is only one question more difficult than the one about the Trinity, and that is this: "What is a concubine?" So a central and vital teaching, yet one which escapes the church's most brilliant minds.

The word "trinity" combines two parts: "tri," meaning three, and "unity," meaning oneness. It is not found in Scripture, but is the best word we have available for expressing the rather puzzling biblical position that God is one, that God is three persons (Father, Son, and Spirit), and that each person is fully God. Logically, of course, these three ideas cannot be held together and in my experience, as soon as anyone claims to have understood it, he or she has already distorted it. I guess this is true of every Trinity illustration you have ever heard. Ice, water, steam; but then God is three persons at once. An egg shell, egg white, and egg yolk; but then each person is fully God. A father, a son, and the relationship between them; but there is only one God. The fact is, our minds are incapable of understanding the mystery of the three-in-one God.

For an arrogant species that has invented space travel and nuclear fission and Marmite and income tax, this may come as a nasty shock, but it is hardly surprising. We cannot even get our minds round optical illusions—how the same image can show both an old woman and a young woman at the same time, yet with no one able to see them both at once—so it should not bother us that we cannot get our minds round the living God. Personally, I am unable even to understand lots of everyday things, like time, and memory, and electricity, never mind infinity and irrational numbers and Immanuel Kant. My mind is hopelessly limited, and even on a good day can only go for about fourteen hours before it needs a rest, so no wonder the mysteries of Yahweh are a little out of my league. "Can you find out the deep things of God? Can you find out the limit of the Almighty?" (Job 11:7).

Just because we cannot understand the Trinity, though, does not mean we should not study it. It is of huge importance. Not only does it humble us by showing how small we are, it reveals things about the character of God that we would not otherwise know. For instance, it shows us that God is in community. Think about it: There is a loving relationship at the heart of the universe. Yahweh did not create man because he was lonely! He had been eternally rejoicing in himself, each person of the Trinity in the others, like a fountain that is so bubbling with water that it overflows and brings life to all around it. That is why the creatures made in his image also live in community. We echo our Creator.

It shows us that authority, also, is found in the Trinity. The Father sent the Son, the Father and the Son sent the Spirit, and the Spirit seeks to honor them, not himself:

"He will not speak on his own authority, but whatever he hears he will speak ... All that the Father has is mine; therefore I said that he will take what is mine and declare it to you" (John 16:13, 15).

It is an unfashionable idea today, but the clear authority structure in the Trinity is the foundation for authority within marriage and the church (1 Cor. 11:3). But it is also important for its own sake, because it reveals a God who is sacrificial and submissive and self-giving in and of himself, not just because we exist. Human sin, in requiring salvation, did not force God to change his eternal nature. It provided an opportunity for him to publicly parade that eternal nature to everyone and everything he had made.

Finally, it shows us that God is personal, but in a higher and greater and more meaningful way than we are. I cannot provide a better explanation of this idea than that of C. S. Lewis:

On the human level one person is one being, and any two persons are two separate beings—just as, in two dimensions (say on a flat sheet of paper) one square is one figure, and any two squares are two separate figures. On the Divine level you still find personalities; but up there you find them combined in new ways which we, who do not live on that level, cannot imagine. In God's dimension, so to speak, you find a being who is three Persons while remaining one Being, just as a cube is six squares while remaining one cube. Of course we cannot fully conceive a Being like that: just as, if we were so made that we perceived only two dimensions in space we could never properly imagine a cube. But we can get a sort of faint notion of it. And when we do, we are then, for the first time in our lives, getting some positive idea, however faint, of something super-personal—something more than a person.[1]

In Jesus' baptism in Mark 1, you can see all of these things actually happening. You can see the submission of the Son, the encouragement of the Spirit, and the affirmation of the Father all coming together. You can see a demonstration of relationship and authority and unity and personality all at once. And not only that, but you can also rejoice in the fact that you worship an incomprehensible three-in-one God, a cube in a world of flat squares, a harmony in a world of melodies, a different type of being from anything that is or could ever be conceived.

God in three persons, blessed Trinity!

Endnote
1. C. S. Lewis, Mere Christianity *(London: Collins, 1952)*, 137–38.

HE WHO RAISED JESUS FROM THE DEAD
• • • • • •

If the Spirit of him who raised Jesus from the dead dwells in
you, he who raised Christ Jesus from the dead will also give life
to your mortal bodies through his Spirit who dwells in you.
—Romans 8:11

It's fine to understand the Trinity in theory, but the resurrection shows
them in action. It is a wonderful yet confusing concept: We have Christ
Jesus raised from the dead by the Father, made alive by the Spirit, and
then sending the Spirit (who in verse 9 of this passage is also called
"the Spirit of God" and "the Spirit of Christ") to live in his people and
raise them too. If you can get your head around all of that, then you're
a better person than I am. But the one thing that should be clear is that
the resurrection really happened. God is even given a description, the
title "he who raised Christ Jesus from the dead," as a result of it.

This way of referring to God is as old as Christianity. The first

Christian documents, Paul's letters, use this name several times, and make so many references to the resurrection it is almost overwhelming. Christian preaching from Acts onward assured the world that Jesus had been raised from the dead. Often, the historical fact of the resurrection was used as the basis for confrontation, whether with unbelievers (in Acts) or with churches (in Corinthians). It is historically certain that within thirty years of Jesus' death on the cross, there were growing groups of people all around the Mediterranean saying that Jesus had been resurrected. Perhaps the most vital question a skeptic can ever ask is: Were they right?[1]

We certainly start from an empty tomb; even non-Christian historical scholars admit as much.[2] We can be sure of this for three main reasons. First, if the tomb was not empty, then the Christian movement would have been instantly torpedoed just by someone going and getting the body. Second, the Christian story about the bribe to the soldiers (Matt. 28:11–15) would only have been needed if there was a story about soldiers falling asleep, which in turn would only have been needed if the tomb was actually empty and people needed to find a way to explain it. Third, the Christians made the empty tomb central to their early preaching, which would have been a very silly move unless people knew it was true. The empty tomb is as secure a historical fact as we are likely to find.

There are four main theories to explain how this happened, two of which can be ruled out from the start. (1) The authorities, whether Jewish or Roman, stole Jesus' body, and the disciples mistakenly assumed he had been raised, inventing stories of appearances afterward. The reason this is so clearly wrong is that both the Jewish and Roman authorities were, within a short period of time, trying to stop the Christian movement from growing, and if they had stolen his body they would simply have produced it. (2) Jesus did not really die, but fell into some sort of unconscious state, then revived in the tomb, and moved the stone himself. This is even more ridiculous, if you know anything about Roman crucifixion. Soldiers executed hundreds of people a year, they knew exactly what they were doing, and no one could survive it, far less roll away a two-ton stone and then take out two guards: "It is noticeable that even those historians who are passionately committed to denying the resurrection do not attempt to go by this route … The only other thing worth pointing out about this theory is its remarkable self-reference: though frequently given the *coup de grace*, it keeps reviving itself—carrying about as much conviction as a battered but revived Jesus would have done."[3]

(3) The disciples stole the body, and then pretended to have seen him alive afterward. If people are going to say Jesus did not rise from the dead, this is the best option they have. But consider it for a moment. The most obvious problem with it is that many of the witnesses were killed and tortured for their proclamation of Jesus' resurrection, experiences you would be very unlikely to go through with if you had made it up. Of course, people today are martyred for all sorts of strange ideas, but there is a difference: Right-minded people may die for things they can't prove are true, but they won't die for things they *can* prove are *not* true. (This is even clearer when you are dealing with unbelieving skeptics, which is certainly what Paul and James, the brother of Jesus, were.) Then you've got the women finding the body—as much as we don't like it, women were just not acceptable as witnesses to first-century Jews, so if you were

inventing a story about an empty tomb, you would never have women being the ones to find it. Worst of all, the sources we have are unanimous that the disciples were definitely not expecting Jesus to rise from the dead. Option 3 simply does not stack up.

Which only leaves us with (4): that God raised Jesus from the dead. Notice that the argument we have used has not assumed that there is a God—the word wasn't even mentioned—but rather, it has just not assumed that there isn't (which, perhaps, is the main difference between the Christian and the skeptic at this point). We are saying, as a historical conclusion, that there is only one plausible explanation for the empty tomb, let alone the numerous resurrection appearances we know about. And this means that the resurrection, the most wonderful cooperation between Father, Son, and Spirit that has ever been seen, actually happened.

So when we refer to God as "he who raised Jesus from the dead," we are not speculating based on mysticism, but concluding based on evidence. We are founding our faith on a firm fact, that in Jerusalem around AD 30 something happened that changed history forever. God raised Christ Jesus from the dead.

Endnotes

1. The remainder of this reflection is adapted from Andrew Wilson, Deluded by Dawkins? *(Eastbourne, UK: Kingsway, 2007).*

2. Geza Vermes, Jesus the Jew: A Historian's Reading of the Gospels *(London: Collins, 1973), 41: "When every argument has been considered and weighed, the only conclusion acceptable to the historian must be that the opinions of the orthodox, the liberal sympathizer and the critical agnostic alike—and even perhaps of the disciples themselves—are simply interpretations of the one disconcerting fact: namely that the women who set out to pay their last respects to Jesus found to their consternation, not a body, but an empty tomb."*

3. N. T. Wright, The Resurrection of the Son of God *(Minneapolis: Augsburg Fortress Publishers, 2003; London: SPCK, 2002), 709.*

# STOP AND STUDY

The historical fact of the resurrection of Jesus underpins the whole of Christianity. If there is any area of history worth researching in detail, it is this—your life will almost certainly change as a result of seeing the factual foundations of the Christian faith. There are a number of excellent books on the subject, including the following.

Lee Strobel, *The Case for Christ* (Grand Rapids, MI: Zondervan, 1998).

—One of the clearest available presentations of the evidence, as a journalist investigates the evidence surrounding the life, death, and resurrection of Jesus.

Frank Morison, *Who Moved the Stone?* (Grand Rapids, MI: Zondervan, 1987).

—The famous study of the resurrection by a man who came as a skeptic and left as a Christian.

Gary R. Habermas and Michael R. Licona, *The Case for the Resurrection of Jesus* (Grand Rapids, MI: Kregel, 2004).

—One of the world's leading apologists presents the case for the resurrection.

N. T. Wright, *The Resurrection of the Son of God* (London: SPCK, 2002).

—A massive, and brilliantly written, scholarly volume on the resurrection. Sections IV and V are particularly helpful.

William Lane Craig, *The Son Rises: The Historical Evidence for the Resurrection of Jesus* (Chicago: Moody, 1981).

—Another collection of evidence from a leading Christian debater.

Charles Foster, *The Jesus Inquest: The Case for and Against the Resurrection of the Christ* (Oxford: Monarch, 2007).

—A provocative new book that looks at the argument from both sides, and helps both atheists and Christians avoid caricatures of the others' perspective.

YAHWEH IS ONE

· · · · · ·

Hear, O Israel: Yahweh our God, Yahweh is one.
—Deuteronomy 6:4

A lot of radical things have been said about God over the years, but perhaps the most radical of them all was in Deuteronomy 6:4. To us, no doubt, it seems a fairly run-of-the-mill thing to say, the sort of thing religious people sometimes say. That is because we live in a culture dominated by three monotheistic (one-God) religions: Judaism, Christianity, and Islam. But in the world of the fourteenth century BC, it would have been completely out there. The Jews believed it, obviously, but every other civilization was certain, not just that it wasn't true, but that it wasn't even possible—a rather odd and confusing use of words. Let me illustrate.

If someone were to advertise in the paper tomorrow that they were starting a new faith and that they believed God was one, we would shrug our shoulders and move on, having come across things like that before. If instead, though, the advert said they believed God was orange, we might balk, or laugh, but we would probably not know quite what to do with it. If we could establish that they were being serious, we would have to assume either that they were mad, or that they were using the word "god" in a completely different sense to us. This may give us an idea of the strangeness of the Jews' belief in one God.

The nations around Israel at this time all believed in many gods. They might serve only one of them, but if they did, they would never contest the claim that there *were* lots of others. In times of war, when a nation lost, they would then have to worship the gods of their conquerors, as if to signify that their enemy's god was more powerful than theirs. This is what Nebuchadnezzar forced people to do in Daniel 3, and why he was so astonished at the reaction of Shadrach, Meshach, and Abednego. In this sense, the polytheistic (many-God) world of the Old Testament was more characteristic of the way we support football teams than the way we worship; I support Liverpool and you support Newcastle, and we can debate who is better, but I would be regarded as a couple of pork pies short of a picnic if I said that Liverpool was the only football club in existence.

Yet this is what Israel says of Yahweh. Deuteronomy 6:4 was known as the *Shema* (from the first word, meaning "Hear!") and it was a prayer the Jews would recite daily for the next 3,500 years and counting, to remind themselves of the most important truth they had: Their God was the one and only, and the gods of the nations were idols. Yahweh's commands to Israel to destroy cities completely or to avoid foreign wives like the plague may look racist to us today, but compromise in these areas usually led to Israel cobbling together different gods into a polytheistic soup. Yahweh, unlike the gods of the nations, was not content to be the first among equals, or even the greatest of many gods. Rather, he wanted the Israelites to understand that he was the only God, the true King, and the gods of the nations were not gods at all:

"Know therefore today, and lay it to your heart, that Yahweh is God in heaven above and on the earth beneath; there is no other" (Deut. 4:39).

"Therefore you are great, O Yahweh God. For there is none like you, and there is no God besides you, according to all that we have heard with our ears" (2 Sam. 7:22).

"For all the gods of the peoples are worthless idols, but Yahweh made the heavens" (Ps. 96:5).

"Is there a God besides me? There is no Rock; I know not any. All who fashion idols are nothing" (Isa. 44:8–9).

This truth was what the *Shema* was originally all about. It was not originally about the nature of Yahweh's being—how many pieces or even persons there were to God—although the rabbis in the first century, as they do today, used it in that sense to debate with Christians.[1] (In fact, Old Testament Jews seemed to have no problem speaking of various ways in which Yahweh revealed himself—Law [torah], Glory [*shekinah*], Wisdom, Word, and Spirit—and the statement that God did not consist of different aspects was hardly worth making the foundation of their entire religion.) No: The oneness of God was about his uniqueness, his only-ness, his sovereignty, the utter difference between him and every other being, whether worshipped or not.

This is a vital truth for the Christian church. There is no room to compromise over the one-ness of God, not with atheists, or polytheists (like Hindus), or monotheists (like Muslims). Zealous Jews were prepared to face all sorts of terrible consequences for saying "apart from you there is no God" in a pagan culture, and we must be too. Although it sometimes looks as if it has the ring of acceptability, the truth that there is one God, and only one God, is a dangerous one, with a history of burnt corpses and severed heads to prove it. But it is also a wonderful one, for it shows the false gods for what they really aren't, and the true God for who he really is.

No other God but you, Lord!

Endnote
1. This point is made by N. T. Wright, The New Testament and the People of God *(Minneapolis: Ausburg Fortress Press, 1996; London: SPCK, 1992), 259.*

GOD OUR FATHER

· · · · · ·

When Israel was a child, I loved him, and out of Egypt I called
my son. The more they were called, the more they went away;
they kept sacrificing to the Baals and burning offerings to idols.
Yet it was I who taught Ephraim to walk; I took them up by
their arms, but they did not know that I healed them.
—Hosea 11:1–3

They say familiarity breeds contempt, and we are so used to the idea of God
being our Father that we have become casual about it. Not only that, but
the world, whether through our personal experience or through the media,
consistently erodes our understanding of fatherhood, so that the word may
suggest a violent monster, or a lazy slob, or an effeminate man, or simply
a faceless and unknown biological parent. We need to rediscover what the
Bible means by the word "father." So in this reflection we're going to look at
a number of things that having God as our Father actually means.

(1) God our Father is our source of life. This, unlike all the other things fatherhood means in Scripture, is true for everyone, whether or not they are disciples. In Acts 17:28, Paul tells even the idolatrous pagans in Athens, "We are indeed his offspring" (although it is significant that he uses the word offspring, which does not imply the relationship connected with the word children). Just as no one has ever been born without an earthly father, so everyone in history owes their existence to God.

(2) God our Father adopts us into his family. This is shocking! We were not the princes and princesses, born into relationship with the King and always destined for royalty ourselves. We were the street kids, foul-smelling and foul-mouthed orphans, with no royalty, no rights, and certainly no relationship; yet one day the King walked up to us, and chose us to join him in the palace, giving us all these things in the process—and all his inheritance as well! "So you are no longer a slave, but a son, and if a son, then an heir through God" (Gal. 4:7).

(3) God our Father gives us the family likeness. Humans are powerless to do this, of course; if an Afro-Caribbean couple adopt a white child, the child does not suddenly look like her parents. But with God, this is just what happens. Rather than leaving us as we were, looking out of place in the divine family, God "predestined [us] to be conformed to the image of his Son, in order that he might be the firstborn among many brothers" (Rom. 8:29). As we grow in his family, we take on more and more of the family likeness and, amazingly, people who know God start telling us that we look just like our Father.

(4) God our Father knows our every need, and provides for us. Would you give your kids a rock if they asked for a sandwich, or a

rattlesnake if they wanted fish fingers? You can almost hear the sarcasm in Jesus' voice as he confronts people with the reality of a truly loving Father, a Father who knows every hair on our head (all eighty thousand of them if you've got a full complement), and to whom all things belong. This doesn't mean we get everything we want—I meet very few parents who give their children everything they want, and those who do end up with very spoiled children. But it does mean that everything we need will be taken care of by our heavenly Father.

(5) God our Father disciplines us. This is less popular, but it is so crucial that Hebrews says, "If you are left without discipline, in which all have participated, then you are illegitimate children and not sons" (Heb. 12:8). People who do not face discipline become like lepers, unable to feel pain resulting from their behavior, and end up destroying themselves and others. If Yahweh had not disciplined Israel, they would have slid into idolatry and never come out again; if Jesus had not disciplined Peter, who knows how his pride and temper might have destroyed the early church? As much as we may find it uncomfortable, God disciplines us, and that is a good sign. As a wise pastor I know once said, it's when your Father stops disciplining you that you're in real trouble.

(6) God our Father is desperately compassionate toward us, despite our sins. Scripture is overflowing with examples—think of the prodigal father, pelting down the road to kiss his philandering, squandering, selfish son—but for me the most moving is in the passage we began with in Hosea 11. Think of a father, carefully and lovingly nurturing his child, but finding that the more love he shows, the further away from him his child drifts. As time goes on, the child rejects

the love and authority of the Father completely, at some points even calling himself the child of another person. Yet the Father, as much as he wants to disown and abandon the child forever, is constrained by a passionate love that cannot be broken: "Yet it was I who taught Ephraim to walk; I took them up by their arms." The compassion and love of the Father are beyond rupture, and so, as God exclaims in verse 8, he cannot simply destroy Israel, and give them up. His Father heart toward them is too strong.

What a picture. The God of Mount Sinai, of thunderstorms and clouds and smoke and awe, teaching his children to walk. We sway from side to side, without balance, and then fall flat on our faces; but God knew we would. He just picks us up and lets us have another go, and another, and another. And even when we should know better, and we grieve our Abba Father, we will be admonished, but never abandoned; disciplined, but never destroyed.

How deep is the love the Father has lavished on us "that we should be called children of God!" (1 John 3:1). And that is what we are.

THE MOTHER OF COMPASSION
• • • • • •

Can a woman forget her nursing child, that she should
have no compassion on the son of her womb? Even
these may forget, yet I will not forget you.
—Isaiah 49:15

Yahweh does not have a gender. He is spirit, neither male nor female. But to make him comprehensible to us, he is often pictured in gender-specific language: as a father, or a husband, or (as here in Isaiah 49) as a mother. This verse does not mean he is female, any more than the Lord's prayer means he is male. Nor does it mean we should talk about him as a "she"—the Bible writers use masculine pronouns for God, and so does Jesus, so we should too. But it does mean that there is an aspect of his character we can see more clearly by talking about him using the image of a woman, just as there are aspects we can see by calling him a "rock" or a "hiding place" or a "shield," without thinking this makes him an "it." That aspect is compassion.

We as humans have four types of compassion. The most common type is *momentary* compassion. This is the feeling I got when I picked up the newspaper this morning and saw pictures of bodies severed by a bomb blast in Mumbai. Animals do not have the capacity to feel sorrow on behalf of creatures they do not know, but people do, and we feel it whenever we turn on the news. Yet this type of compassion does not bring us to action. I am not going to live differently as a result of the feeling I experienced on picking up the paper this morning. In this sense, my compassion is limited; it is not very noble, but momentary, and therefore totally unlike God's.

Sometimes, though, compassion does compel us to action. Usually, this is *merited* compassion. It's what causes us to give to UNICEF to feed starving children in Africa: We see people who deserve better, we feel their pain, and we want to help them. But this compassion, also, is limited, because it only extends to those who (in our view) deserve it. My wife, Rachel, is currently working for a human rights organization, and she was talking recently about how hard it is to motivate people about prison conditions; she remarked that people want to see pictures of helpless babies and rescued child prostitutes, not prisoners. We all distinguish—subconsciously or not—between people who deserve compassion and people who don't. Fortunately this type of compassion, too, is unlike God's. Where would we be if only those who deserved compassion received it?

Occasionally we will experience *missional* compassion. This is where we know that people are difficult, that they may not "deserve" it like the next person, and that they may not give much back, but we still show them compassion, because we are driven by a purpose, a mission, which enables us to overlook many of their failings. Aid workers, community and social workers, and often health professionals fall into this category—the nine-year-old runaway who swears at everyone and smashes things is harder to love than the sweet, wide-eyed one, but we find ourselves able to persevere, because we have a wider mission (our job, our church, the child's family, or whatever). Yet even this is not like God's compassion, for unlike him, all of us have a breaking point—there are only so many times we can be ignored, rejected, or verbally abused before we leave that person and help someone who will let themselves be helped. Compassion driven by mission and not by relationship will not cope with continual rejection.

The only thing that will is *maternal* compassion. It is hard to think of a person who gives less back than a young child. Screaming in the middle of the night, totally self-absorbed, making mess everywhere, needing twenty-four-hour care, spreading carefully prepared food all over the table, throwing tantrums in the supermarket, biting younger brothers and sisters, and all this without so much as a thank you—yet there is a bond, a relationship, between the two that means the mother continues to have compassion on the child. Mothers of children, and even more so of teenagers, face continual rejection, verbal abuse, and anger from their children, but they remain compassionate. Just watch a mother react to her children being victimized, or the lengths to which she will go to protect them.

This is the picture the Bible uses of Yahweh's compassion for Israel. A rebellious, stubborn, and selfish people, idolatrous and fickle,

THE MOTHER OF COMPASSION

irresponsible and sinful, always rejecting and rarely respecting their creator—no amounts of momentary, or merited, or even missional compassion would be sufficient to maintain relationship and love for them (or for their equally sinful successors, you and me). Only the compassion of a mother for her nursing child is enough. In fact, God says, not even this fully explains it, because there have always been mothers who can abandon their children. So he reminds them, "Even though these may forget, I will not forget you."

We have all witnessed this. I have seen the motherly compassion of God restoring couples who had done everything in their power to ruin their marriages; rescuing backsliders who had run as far away from him as they could; setting free from addictions those who had lived their entire lives without God; and of course continuing to forgive me for the lies and lust and laziness I repeatedly give in to. Like tiny children, we often do all we can to make our parents abandon us. But we have a mother of such infinite compassion that we will never be forgotten.

JESUS CHRIST

· · · · · ·

The beginning of the gospel of Jesus Christ, the Son of God.
—Mark 1:1

Sometimes a name is all you need. In the English-speaking world, names very rarely mean anything; my wife's name is Rachel Wilson, but she is neither a female sheep, nor a son of William (or of anyone else). In the Pitcairn Islands in the South Pacific, though, names have more significance. A day's exploring might lead you up the *Hill of Difficulty*, toward the pagan idol graveyard *Down the god*, or around the threatening sea cliffs *Johnny Fall*, *Where Dan Fall*, and *Where Freddy Fall*. If you were a particularly adventurous cliff walker, you might encounter the more ominously named *Oh Dear*, or my personal favorite, the abrupt *Tom Off.* The names tell you all you need to know.

So it is with Jesus Christ. Lots of people think that "Christ" is Jesus' surname, and few today know what "Jesus" actually means, but a first-century Jew, reading the opening sentence of Mark's gospel would have understood exactly what Mark was claiming about this man. If we are not to miss out, we need to look beneath the surface to see what it was.

The name Jesus was common enough. Quite a lot of Jewish boys were called that, just like a lot of boys in Mexico today are called José or Jésus. But this Jewish boy was called that for a very specific reason. Jesus was the Greek form of the Hebrew name Yeshua, which means "Yahweh saves," and the angel made it very clear to Joseph that he was to be given this name because "he will save his people from their sins" (Matt. 1:21). In other words, the salvation of Israel would take place through this one individual. His name "Yahweh saves," or perhaps "God to the rescue," reflected this destiny.

And there was more to it than that. Another Yeshua, whom we know as Joshua, was the man who had led Israel into the Promised Land. The era of Joshua's leadership had been the period to which centuries of prophecies had been pointing forward, the time of inheritance gained and promises fulfilled, of rescue and great joy for Israel. The age of Jesus' leadership, as Gabriel and Mary and Simeon and Anna proclaim in the first few chapters of Luke, was the same sort of time, only more so. So when Jesus was baptized by John, it was not the first time a Jewish leadership prophet called Yeshua had walked into the Jordan River to enact the salvation of Yahweh in fulfillment of the promise to Abraham. It was just the first time it had been accompanied by an announcement from the throne of heaven itself.

If the name Jesus was normal, though, "Christ" was anything but. Christ was a title; the Greek translation of the Hebrew Messiah, which meant "anointed one." It was the title the Jews used to refer to the coming King, the one in the line of David who would restore the kingdom to Israel. The Jews expected the Christ, among other things, to be a national ruler, to defeat Israel's enemies (at that point, Rome) through military battle, and to usher in the eternal supremacy of Israel over the nations around it, centered around the presence of Yahweh in the Temple. David had done all of these things, winning numerous military victories, expanding Israel's borders, and preparing for the building of the Temple in Jerusalem. The Christ, they reasoned, would do all of this, but in a more definitive and dramatic way.

Jesus did none of them, or at least not in the sense anyone was expecting. He was rejected by a lot of people, for a start. He couldn't even win over his own family, and faced continual opposition from Pharisees, Sadducees, teachers of the law, and the Temple authorities. Far from leading a national army against Rome, he steered clear of violence against them, healed them, and prophesied that they would eventually destroy Jerusalem. He entered the capital on a donkey of humility, not a white horse of triumph, caused uproar in the Temple, and then met an inglorious death outside Jerusalem at the hands of (wait for it) the Romans. It is hard to imagine anyone less fitting of the Jews' picture of a "Christ" than Jesus of Nazareth.

All of this makes it amazing that within twenty years of his death, people all over the known world were referring to him, and worshipping him, as the Christ. To most first-century Jews, calling him "Jesus Christ" was the equivalent of calling me, not "Andrew Wilson" or even "Andrew the preacher," but "Andrew the astronaut"—it was simply an inappropriate title for a crucified prophet. Yet his followers continued using it, and then took their name, Christians, from it. Why?

The answer is simple: They began to realize, largely as a result of the resurrection, that they had misunderstood things, and that in fact Jesus had done exactly what the Messiah was supposed to do. He *was* the anointed King like David, the Son of David, and the King of the Jews. Like David, he was the unlikely hero from an unflattering background, who had been announced to be King by God's prophet (John, who, like Samuel, had been born to a barren woman after a priestly encounter in the Temple). Like David, he had been persecuted by the existing ruler (Herod, who, like Saul, had repeatedly tried to kill the true King). As a result, like David, he had wandered the countryside, keeping a low profile, with his tiny band of loyal followers, before entering Jerusalem to be hailed by the crowds. Like David, he had then conquered Israel's enemies (which ultimately were Satan, sin, and death, not the Romans) once and for all, and been publicly vindicated (through the resurrection). The result was that the worship of Yahweh had gone far further, and the nation of Israel grown far larger, than it ever did under David. This, the disciples realized, is what the word "Christ" really meant.

So when Mark talks about Jesus Christ, he is not just giving you a name. He is telling you that Jesus, the Jew from Nazareth who was crucified by the Romans around AD 30, is both the salvation of his people and the anointed King of Israel. He is saying that Jesus Christ is both Joshua and David, savior and ruler. And whenever you call him that, you are saying it, too.

 WAIT AND WORSHIP

Worshipping Jesus is our purpose, our joy, and our destiny. There are an untold number of good songs and hymns about him which will help you worship, but this hymn, written by Charles Wesley to commemorate the first anniversary of his conversion, is exceptional. Don't just read the words; find a suitable place and sing it out loud. It will build you up in your spirit, as well as honoring God.

O for a thousand tongues to sing
My great Redeemer's praise,
The glories of my God and King,
The triumphs of His grace!

Jesus! the name that charms our fears,
That bids our sorrows cease;
'Tis music in the sinner's ears,
'Tis life, and health, and peace.

He breaks the power of canceled sin,
He sets the prisoner free;

His blood can make the foulest clean,
His blood availed for me.

He speaks, and, listening to His voice,
New life the dead receive,
The mournful, broken hearts rejoice,
The humble poor believe.

Hear Him, ye deaf; His praise, ye dumb,
Your loosened tongues employ;
Ye blind, behold your Savior come,
And leap, ye lame, for joy.

Look unto Him, ye nations, own
Your God, ye fallen race;
Look, and be saved through faith alone,
Be justified by grace.

My gracious Master and my God,
Assist me to proclaim,
To spread through all the earth abroad
The honors of Thy name.

JESUS CHRIST IS LORD

• • • • • •

Therefore God has highly exalted him and bestowed on him the name
that is above every name, so that at the name of Jesus every knee should
bow, in heaven and on earth and under the earth, and every tongue
confess that Jesus Christ is Lord, to the glory of God the Father.
—Philippians 2:9–11

Four words can change the world. They can incite revolutions and shape centuries. "No taxation without representation" practically established America. More people than can be counted have died fighting under a banner of four words: "No king but God!" "Long live the Emperor!" "Live free or die!" What language would the French be speaking without "They shall not pass," or the British without "We shall never surrender"? Or where would American civil rights be without "I have a dream"? When you look back across history, many of the most powerful and subversive things that have ever been said have been four simple words. But no four words in recorded time have been more revolutionary, dangerous, subversive, and civilization-forming than these: "Jesus Christ is Lord."

They may not seem dangerous in the West today. Over time, the explosive four-word rallying cry can become domesticated and lose its original meaning: Witness the way the statements above have become marketing slogans, state mottos, and bumper stickers. For much of history, though, "Jesus Christ is Lord" has been the most dangerous thing you can say, and in many parts of the world today, it still is. This is because it has two extremely radical implications.

First, if Jesus Christ is Lord, then no one else is. This is the clearest meaning the phrase would have had in the first century: Jesus is Lord, therefore Caesar is not. Remember, the early church did not live in a democracy where everyone could say pretty much what they liked. They lived as subjects of a pagan ruler in a context of imperial worship, where signs of undermining the emperor's authority were quickly recognized and brutally squashed, usually by crucifixion. Declaration of the lordship of Jesus, as opposed to that of Caesar, was therefore not a harmless religious statement, but a subversive political one.

The closest equivalent we have in recent times is probably Communism. In our lifetime, numerous Russian and Chinese Christians have died and been imprisoned because of this obvious truth: If Jesus Christ is Lord, then the Communist Party is not. In 1972, twenty-year-old Ivan Moiseyev joined those who, by their lives and deaths, showed that the lordship of Jesus could not be shared: "'I will never agree to remain silent about God.' ... His commanders continued to interrogate him, trying to get him to deny Jesus. They put him in refrigerated cells. They clothed him in a special rubber suit, into which they pumped air until his chest was so compressed he could hardly breathe.... A few days later, his body was returned to his family. It showed that he had been stabbed six times around the heart. He had wounds on his head and around the mouth. There were signs of beatings on the whole body. Then he had been drowned."[1]

Ivan Moiseyev, like thousands of others from Stephen onward, was killed because of four words: Jesus Christ is Lord. We can believe those words, but it is only when we are prepared to die for them that we really know what they mean. If Jesus is Lord, then no one else is.

The second implication is even worse—that Jesus Christ is Yahweh. The Greek word used here for Lord, *kurios*, was the word the Jews used throughout the Greek Old Testament to translate Yahweh. Now, this on its own doesn't prove Paul was saying Jesus is Yahweh; the word lord could also mean master, or even just sir. But if you look at the context, you will see that this is exactly what he is saying. Time and again, including here, Paul takes standard Old Testament passages about Yahweh, and turns them into passages about Jesus:

Old Testament	New Testament
Hear O Israel: *Yahweh our God, Yahweh is one.* (Deut. 6:4)	For us *there is one God,* the Father, from whom are all things and for whom we exist, and *one Lord, Jesus Christ,* through whom are all things and through whom we exist. (1 Cor. 8:6)
And it shall come to pass that *everyone who calls on the name of Yahweh shall be saved.* (Joel 2:32)	If you confess with your mouth that Jesus is Lord and believe in your heart that God raised him from the dead, you will be saved … For *"everyone who calls on the name of the Lord will be saved."* (Rom. 10:9, 13)

For I am God, and there is no other. By myself I have sworn; from my mouth has gone out in righteousness a word that shall not return: *"To me every knee shall bow, every tongue shall swear allegiance."* (Isa. 45:22–23)	Therefore God has highly exalted him and bestowed on him the name that is above every name, so that at the name of Jesus *every knee should bow,* in heaven and on earth and under the earth, and *every tongue confess* that <u>Jesus Christ is Lord</u>, to the glory of God the Father. (Phil. 2:9–11)

What an astonishing thing to be claiming: that Jesus of Nazareth is Yahweh. Just as astonishing is the fact that the (Jewish) early Christians did not for a minute think that this made Jesus a sort of "second god," or that there had suddenly become two or even three gods. They vigorously argued that there was one God—not least in the passages we have just quoted—but they also argued that Jesus was this one God, the Lord of the world, Yahweh made flesh. And so he is.

So when Paul says that Jesus has been given the name that is above every name, this is what he is talking about. Jesus Christ has been given the name above every earthly ruler, caesar, or president, but also above every heavenly power or authority. Jesus Christ is the one before whom all people must bow, whatever the consequences, but he is also Yahweh himself, God made man, crucified in magnificent obedience and therefore exalted in glorious magnificence.

Or, in four words: Jesus Christ is Lord!

Endnote
1. DC Talk, Live Like a Jesus Freak *(Minneapolis: Bethany, 2001),* 44–49.

THE WORD BECAME FLESH

• • • • • •

And the Word became flesh and tabernacled among us.
—John 1:14 (Literal Translation Version)

You have just read perhaps the most outrageous sentence in history. No truth ever revealed, no truth, is more jarring than the fact that the Word, the pre-existent Son of God, became human and set up the tent of his dwelling among people. There are lots of important truths in the gospel, but they all depend on this one. The cross made possible freedom from sin, and the resurrection secured it, but the writing was on the wall the day Mary got pregnant. It is not exaggeration to say that the incarnation—God becoming flesh—is the most scandalous teaching anyone has ever given. More scandalously, it is completely true.

Take it a bit at a time. John talks quite a lot about "the Word" in this chapter, and shows his Jewish readers several things about him. In verse 1, we hear he is eternal ("In the beginning was the Word"),

distinct from God ("and the Word was with God") and yet God himself ("and the Word was God"). He was, with God, responsible for the
whole of creation, and nothing was made without him (v. 3). He is full
of light, life, glory, grace, and truth (vv. 4, 14). So we have an eternal
being through whom everything was created, distinct from God the
Father but at the same time fully God himself.

In and of itself, this was controversial but not outrageous to Jewish readers. They knew of several passages in the Old Testament that
hinted at a plurality of persons within Yahweh: "Let us make man in
our image, after *our* likeness" (Gen. 1:26); "Your throne, *O God*, is
forever and ever. The sceptre of your kingdom is a sceptre of upright-
ness; you have loved righteousness and hated wickedness. Therefore
God, your God, has anointed you" (Ps. 45:6–7); "And I heard the voice
of the Lord saying, 'Whom shall I send, and who will go for *us*?'" (Isa.
6:8); "Yahweh possessed me at the beginning of his work, the first of
his acts of old. Ages ago I was set up, at the first, before the beginning
of the earth" (Prov. 8:22–23).

What was outrageous, though, was the statement that this being,
the Word, had "become flesh." Remember, the Jews had several ways
of speaking about God's interaction with man—Wisdom, Law, Word,
Glory, and Spirit (the last four of which, by the way, are used directly
in this chapter, and the first is alluded to throughout it)—but none
of them involved God becoming a man. How could the transcendent
God become so imminent? How was spirit now body? How could
someone so holy become so humble? To this day, the incarnation, far
more than the crucifixion or resurrection, is the biggest problem Jews
and Muslims have with the gospel.

John uses a metaphor to explain: "and tabernacled among us." The tabernacle was the large, pavilion-like tent in which the presence of God lived when the Israelites were in the desert. The Jews had a way of understanding how Yahweh could be close to his people in a tent, because their history was built on it (and they still worshipped in the tent's successor, the Temple). So John used this as a picture for what the Word was doing: making the presence of Yahweh available to people, by moving in among them. The Son of God, in becoming flesh, was definitively camping with humankind. Only in this "tabernacle" he was no longer obscured by two veils and unapproachable to all but the high priest, but visible and tangible to everyone.

This is the biggest of all miracles. If you stop and think about it, the amazing things Jesus does in the gospels are not at all surprising if you believe in the incarnation. If Jesus was fully God, as John is saying he is (and as Jesus himself says he is in John 8:58), then it would be totally bizarre if the storm didn't go quiet when he told it to. If Jesus really was the Word made flesh, then it would be far stranger if he hadn't risen from the dead than if he had. People who struggle with Easter simply show they haven't understood Christmas.

You see, the incarnation raises the stakes. If people are struggling with the practical implications of the gospel, the incarnation will make things much worse. I have had the privilege, once or twice, of speaking to sicknesses in Jesus' name and seeing them go immediately, as well as seeing literally hundreds of others healed through people far more anointed by God than I am. I often find unbelievers—and believers, for that matter—are amazed that anyone would say God can do this sort of thing. But when faced with the incarnation, those who try to deny God's healing power are like people chasing their pet hamster out of the sitting-room while they ignore the elephant on the sofa. We are saying something far more outrageous, far more foolish to modern man, than that God heals people. We are saying he actually became flesh.

This is breathtaking. Solomon was right to wonder:

"But will God indeed dwell with man on the earth? Behold, heaven and the highest heaven cannot contain you, how much less this house that I have built!" (2 Chron. 6:18).

Yet the answer to his question, of whether or not God will dwell with man on earth, is an emphatic "Yes!" And now he has! The pre-existent Word somehow limited his omnipresence, his everywhere-ness, to become a human like you and me. He who was pure spirit lived in a tent of flesh (and according to Acts 17:31, he still does). The God of all things, for whom nothing is too hard, was made man, in the most outrageous move he could possibly have made.

What a Savior. What a gospel.

THE LION AND THE LAMB

· · · · · ·

And one of the elders said to me, "Weep no more; behold, the
Lion of the tribe of Judah, the Root of David, has conquered,
so that he can open the scroll and its seven seals." And between
the throne and the four living creatures and among the elders
I saw a Lamb standing, as though it had been slain.
—Revelation 5:5–6

It sounds like a strange dream. Revelation is so full of imagery that it gen-
erates the most extreme of responses, from lethargy to *Left Behind*. People
either ignore it, considering it far too confusing to get anything out of, or
they obsess over it, producing all sorts of fancifully detailed predictions
about the end of time. But the main thrust of the book is not to predict
what will happen in the future, at least not until the end. It is to show
disciples what is really happening in the present.[1] It is a series of visions
and metaphors designed to pull back the curtain, and show the readers

(who were originally suffering Christians) the sovereignty of God through history, even when evil looks to be prevailing. Like a cartoon, or even a hologram, it is designed to change people's views, give a heavenly perspective on earthly events, and reveal the one who is in charge of it all. That is why John calls it "the revelation of Jesus Christ" (1:1).

The reason this is important is that the scene we have just read is not in the distant future. It is the way things are now. The throne in 4:2–11 describes the sovereignty of God now, not at some point in the future. The worship God receives from the hosts of heaven in 5:8–14 is what he is receiving now. As disciples in the world today, we are not weeping, waiting for the Root of David to conquer, but being told to "weep no more," because he already has conquered (as Colossians 2:13–15 makes very clear). Creation is not waiting for Christ to be thought worthy to wrap up history, but joyfully acknowledging that he is, and seeing all that happens through that prism. And John's vision of Jesus as the Lion and the Lamb is a perception of what is, not a prediction of what is to come.

A lion needs no introduction. The mane, the enormous strength, the roar that can be heard for miles—everything about it speaks of regal authority and power. So high is the lion above other animals in the food chain that, in the African savannahs, other large predators such as hyenas and cheetahs eat their prey at once, so as to avoid being driven off it by lions. The king of beasts, on the other hand, sits and eats at leisure, even falling asleep next to its meal, safe in the knowledge that no one would dare challenge it. Lions' calm but terrifying authority is obvious to all creatures, humankind included.

It is this authority, with its strength and power, that is suggested by referring to Jesus as the Lion of the tribe of Judah. Like a lion, he is untamable, wild, strong, dominant; an alpha male who would still storms and trash Temple tables. Like a lion, you would be confident of him winning any battle, and would be overwhelmed with fear if you ever crossed him. Imagine provoking a lion to a fight, or (worse) trying to attack its offspring. The true Lion King, roaring from Zion and exerting dominion wherever he puts his feet, is a sight to see. But unlike the four-legged versions, who fight and win for a while but eventually die, this Lion has conquered permanently and definitively, and been given ultimate authority—the only one in history who is considered worthy to open the scroll and its seven seals.

So you can imagine John's surprise when, with all of these images in his mind, he turns to see what the Lion of the tribe of Judah looks like. Personally, I would be preparing to hide under the bed, but John looks and sees "a Lamb standing, as though it had been slain." What a contrast! You cannot imagine a more humble creature, nor any animal less likely to be enthroned as king of all creation, than a lamb, far less a *slain* lamb. Yet that is exactly what John sees. The symbol of kingship and power has given way to one of servanthood and sacrifice. The mighty roar he was anticipating is now a deafening silence. An animal that can rip other creatures to pieces has come in the form of one that gets carved for Sunday lunch. Somehow, this king is in a completely different category from any other.

Now, in the light of the gospel of grace, perhaps it is obvious how Jesus is the Lion of Judah and the Lamb who was slain. But in my experience, most churches and traditions emphasize the slain Lamb, without remembering that he is still the conquering Lion. I know what people are trying to achieve when they describe Jesus the man in terms of helplessness and weakness, and I share their understanding of what becoming human cost him, but these words imply that, once he had decided to come to earth, he was powerless and at the mercy of his enemies. This is not the case:

"Put your sword back in its place ... Do you think that I cannot appeal to my Father, and he will at once send me more than twelve legions of angels? But how then should the Scriptures be fulfilled, that it must be so?" (Matt. 26:52–54).

Throughout his life, even at the cross, he was still the Lion of Judah, sovereign, wild, able at any point to obliterate his enemies with one blast from his mouth.

To me, the powerful thing about this vision isn't the picture of the lion or the lamb, but the fact that Jesus is both. It is when you see that the roaring God of Amos came to earth as the Lamb of God that you understand how wonderful grace really is. It is the very fact that the man on the cross was the Lion of the tribe of Judah, able to destroy anyone, whenever he chose, that makes the crucifixion so amazing. When I watched *The Lion, the Witch and the Wardrobe*, the reason Aslan's death on the stone table moved me so much is not that he couldn't have fought back, but that he could. To paraphrase Schindler's remark to Goeth in *Schindler's List*, "Power is when you can do anything to anybody—and you don't."

Jesus, as the Lion of the tribe of Judah, had all power and kingly strength at his disposal, yet he chose to become the Lamb that was slain. So, as the angels sang in response, "Worthy are you to take the scroll and open its seals!"

Endnote
1. *This has been brilliantly argued by G. K. Beale,* Revelation, *NIGTC (Grand Rapids, MI: Eerdmans), 1999, and is well explained in a more accessible format by John Hosier,* The Lamb, the Beast and the Devil *(Oxford: Monarch), 2002.*

CHRIST JESUS OUR MEDIATOR

• • • • • •

For there is one God, and one mediator between God and
men, the man Christ Jesus, who gave himself as a ransom for
all, which is the testimony given at the proper time.
—1 Timothy 2:5–6

I drove past a bizarre billboard the other day. Rachel and I were on the
New Jersey turnpike when our eyes were caught by a poster screaming, "Amazing Divorce Deals!" Curious as to what on earth it could
be advertising, I read it, and discovered it was selling "mediation ser-
vices," the process by which divorcing couples, rather than suing each
other, reach an agreement outside court through a neutral third party
called a mediator.

Mediation happens because two parties are so far removed from
each other that they cannot resolve things themselves. When neither
side is willing, or able, to concede ground, they require someone

who can represent both sides. Of course, no earthly mediator can fully or perfectly represent either side, let alone both of them, so what you end up with is a compromise—not completely satisfactory to anyone, but much better than the loss of money and loss of face that result from a court case. Imperfect mediators inevitably produce imperfect solutions.

Job needed a mediator between him and God. He had lost his children and his possessions, and was in such pain from the boils on his skin he was scraping himself with broken pottery. He wanted to dispute with God, to debate whether or not he deserved the extreme suffering he was experiencing, but realized how far beneath God he was, and cried out in frustration: "For He is not a man, as I am, that I may answer Him, and that we should go to court together. Nor is there any mediator between us, who may lay his hand on us both" (Job 9:32–33 NKJV).

What a profound statement in the midst of such suffering! "There is no mediator between us." How could man and God ever face each other across a courtroom? Or how could anyone mediate for them, representing the two of them simultaneously? God is so vastly different from man that anyone who could speak for one of them could not possibly speak for the other. So Job remains without access to God, without anyone to fight his corner, stalemated—or checkmated!—by his humanity, God's divinity, and the chasm between the two.

The problem is fundamental: To mediate properly between God and man, you would actually have to be both God and man. To be a top interpreter for the Chinese embassy, it is not enough just to speak both Chinese and English; you have to be both Chinese and English (by having been brought up in a bilingual household). It is the same with being both God and man. And since no person can become God, the only way that Job or Jeremiah or you could ever have a mediator between you and God is if God himself became man.

Enter "the man Christ Jesus." What a solution! Fully God, completely holy and glorious and untainted and pure, hating sin and loving righteousness as much as God the Father, and with all authority on heaven and earth given to him; yet also fully man, experiencing as much temptation and suffering and rejection as any human ever has, sympathizing with our weaknesses and knowing our frailties (Heb. 4:15). At last, we have a mediator who can perfectly represent God to man and man to God.

Yet there is no compromise. Unlike the divorce mediator, Jesus does not haggle on man's behalf, persuading God that a little bit of sin is justifiable due to the weakness of human flesh. On the contrary, he does not remove one iota of God's law, and in fact raises the standard (Matt. 5:17–48; this passage is a good response to people in the media who think moral standards are Old Testament and Jesus is fluffy). Nor does Jesus smite everyone down on God's behalf for being impure, which—since we are 100 percent responsible for the divorce—he has every right to do. There is no maneuvering, no give-and-take, and therefore there are no disgruntled parties leaving the courtroom complaining that they didn't get a fair deal.

Instead, he mediates by including the guilty party (us) in himself, fulfilling the law on our behalf in his life, and then reconciling us to God in his death. It is as though the divorce lawyer were able to incorporate the selfish, adulterous husband into himself, overcome all his weaknesses in a magnificent display of masculinity and love, remove the husband's failures permanently by dying himself, and then present the husband back to his wife perfect, thus restoring the marriage. The sacrifice and love that would be required to do this, in human terms, are unthinkable. But that, and far more, is what it took Jesus to bring us back into relationship with God.

There is one God, and one mediator between God and men: the man Christ Jesus.

PAUSE AND PRAY

We can only approach God because Jesus is our mediator. We don't approach God through angels, or through Mary, or priests, or pastors, but through Jesus alone. So when we sin, it is through Jesus alone that we are able to be restored, cleansed, and forgiven. As John puts it in 1 John 2:1, "If anyone does sin, we have an advocate with the Father, Jesus Christ the righteous. He is the propitiation for our sins, and not for ours only but also for the sins of the whole world."

You may want to take this opportunity to confess your sins to God, and thank him for the forgiveness that he offers through Christ Jesus our mediator.

> *Almighty God, our heavenly Father,*
> *we have sinned against you and against our fellow men,*
> *in thought and word and deed,*
> *through negligence, through weakness,*
> *through our own deliberate fault.*
> *We are truly sorry,*
> *and repent of all our sins.*

For the sake of your Son Jesus Christ, who died for us,
forgive us all that is past;
and grant that we may serve you in newness of life
to the glory of your name. Amen.

JESUS SHINES

• • • • • •

His face was like the sun shining in full strength. When
I saw him, I fell at his feet as though dead.
—Revelation 1:16–17

Ask a four-year-old to draw a picture of his dad, and the odds are you will get amusing results. It might, possibly, look something like a person, but it will be hopelessly limited. Everything will be out of proportion, there will be lots of things missing, lots of misunderstandings (arms coming out of the side of the head, for instance), and it will be in two dimensions, not three. A child of that age is simply unable to draw something as complex as a human body.

Most of us, if asked to describe Jesus, would do the same. We might talk about the baby in a manger, particularly if it's Christmas. We might describe the teacher on the mountainside in Galilee, surrounded by sheep and people. We might picture a sorrowful face peering down from a wooden cross. We might imagine the ascension, a mysterious figure levitating off a mountainside in a long white dressing-gown. But each of these, although helpful in some ways, is hopelessly limiting. An adult of this present age is simply unable to picture something as glorious as the risen Jesus.

So John helps us. John knew Jesus the man and saw him teach, eat, fish, heal, and die. But he, his brother, and Peter were blown away when they became "eyewitnesses of his majesty" (2 Peter 1:16), catching something of Jesus' incredible splendor when he was transfigured before them. Here in Revelation, at the end of his life, John describes an even more astonishing vision of Jesus Christ, including eyes like flames of fire, a voice like thundering waters, and so on. And he concludes by saying, "His face was like the sun shining in full strength."

Just think for a minute about what it means for Jesus to be compared to the sun. The sun is unthinkably massive, containing more than 99.8 percent of the total mass of the entire solar system. Most of the remaining 0.2 percent is taken up by Jupiter, a planet which is itself 318 times the size of the earth; and on this earth, you are just one six-billionth of the population, separated from everyone else by oceans, mountains, and 6,800 languages. In other words, compared with you, the sun is fairly large.

But now consider what it means for Jesus' face to be "like the sun shining in full strength." The light of the sun has been sustaining every form of life on the planet for its entire history. So has Jesus, only more so. The sun is so dazzling that we cannot look at it without being blinded, even though we are nearly 100 million miles away. So is Jesus, only more so. The sun is so bright that every year, simply

INCOMPARABLE

by shining upon cold and barren places, it causes life and growth to burst forth where previously there was empty wilderness. So does Jesus, only more so. The sun is so powerful that in one second, it emits more energy than we humans have generated in all of human history: 92 billion one-megaton nuclear bombs, every second. So does Jesus, only more so.

We must fight to remember this, in a world (and a church culture) where Jesus is often depicted as a helpless baby or a dying victim, and where he is often thought of as a teacher or a friend. He is those things. But if you asked John, his best friend who traveled and ate and relaxed and worked with him, what Jesus was like, he would point you to Revelation 1, and the most frightening, awe-inspiring picture of anyone you will ever see.

How do we see Jesus—do we have a mature view of him, or a four-year-old's drawing? One test is this: When we spend time with him, what is our response? Perhaps we study his teaching, while adjusting it to fit our theology. Perhaps we get excited by his offer of forgiveness, while not changing our behavior. Perhaps we chat to him like we would to a friend, but without any sense of awe or reverence. My guess is this: If we truly see him as he is now, as John saw him, with "his face shining like the sun in full strength," then we will probably react like John did.

"When I saw him, I fell at his feet as though dead."

KING OF KINGS AND LORD OF LORDS

· · · · · ·

*Then I saw heaven opened, and behold, a white horse! The
one sitting on it is called Faithful and True, and in righteousness he judges and makes war ... On his robe and on his thigh
he has a name written, King of kings and Lord of lords.*
—Revelation 19:11, 16

Let me tell you about the most humiliating moment of my adult life.
I used to work in London for a firm of strategy consultants, most of
whom were high-powered people who worked extremely hard and got
paid a lot of money. One evening I was working late and rang my friend
Tom, from upstairs, to see if he wanted to take a break outside. He did,
so I walked toward the stairs to go down, when suddenly an idea hit
me. By hiding in the elevator alcove in the stairwell, I could leap out
and scare the living daylights out of Tom when he walked past me. No
one else was around, and he would be coming down any minute. Sure

enough, within seconds I heard the third floor door swing open and footsteps coming down the stairs. I waited until he was within about a yard of my hiding place, and then jumped out with a massive shout, causing him to fly backward into the wall, yelling with fright. It was only then that I realized: It wasn't Tom. Tom had taken the elevator. It was a principal of the firm, a very senior man with a six-figure salary and the right to fire me. I received a severe reprimand, as you would expect, and never worked with him again.

Those moments when you suddenly realize who somebody is can be devastating. Drama is built on it: King Oedipus and his mother; King Lear and his daughter; King Richard and the Sheriff of Nottingham; King Kong and the nameless person who accidentally steps on his foot. The more powerful the person, the worse it is to find out that you have not been treating him or her with proper respect. So it is not surprising that the most devastating moment of them all will be when the King of Kings and Lord of Lords is shown for who he is.

The biblical word for this is "revelation." The Greek word has the sense of unveiling, disclosure, even dénouement—that moment in the story when you finally realize who someone is, and what it means. No earthly stories can prepare us for what this will be like, because King Richard and King Kong are laughable in comparison to King Jesus. But there are a number of times in Scripture when Yahweh is suddenly seen to be the God of gods, and the Bible suggests that the return of Jesus will be something like these.

The Philistines see it in 1 Samuel 5. They capture the ark of Yahweh, but they then make the mistake of putting it next to their god, Dagon. This is a chronic mismatch, the equivalent of that scene in

Jurassic Park when they put the goat in the tyrannosaurus paddock. Next morning, they find Dagon face down before the ark of Yahweh. Their response is comic:

> So they took Dagon and put him back in his place. But when they rose early on the next morning, behold, Dagon had fallen face downward on the ground before the ark of Yahweh, and the head of Dagon and both his hands were lying cut off on the threshold. (1 Sam. 5:3–4)

And thus begins the original "hot potato" story, as the Philistines send the ark to Gath, then Ekron, with destruction coming upon them wherever it goes. Eventually, they realize that they are dealing with the God of gods, and in fear they hurriedly send it back to Israel.

The Baal worshippers see it in 1 Kings 18. When challenged by Elijah to decide who is the true God—Yahweh or Baal—the Israelites say nothing. So the prophet devises a challenge: Whoever sends down fire from heaven to consume their sacrifice, he is the true God. Baal, of course, manages nothing in several hours, but Yahweh utterly consumes the offering, the soaking wet wood, the dust, and even the stones (1 Kings 18:38). Like burglars who discover they have robbed the mafia chieftain's home by mistake, the Israelites suddenly appreciate who they have got on the wrong side of, and fall face down in terror and worship, crying, "Yahweh is God!"

We could go on. Pharaoh, Og, Goliath, Ahab, Sennacherib, Nebuchadnezzar, Darius, Herod—Scripture describes numerous times when pagans, often too late, realize that they are not just up against any "god," but the King of Kings and the Lord of Lords. The revelation of Jesus, though, will be more dramatic even than these. You see, that list of pagans knew that they were opposing a God of some sort, even if they didn't realize how powerful he was. Their theology, as confused as it was, at least led them to believe that if God stood against them, they were in trouble.

But when Jesus is revealed, it will be a shock to almost everyone (1 Thess. 5:2–5). People will be expecting a teacher with eyes of blue and the voice of a soothing brook, not a ruler with eyes of fire and the voice of a raging torrent. They will be proclaiming "peace and security," and be met with one "who judges and makes war." The Jesus they are flippant about, humbly riding a donkey, will be replaced with one they are frightened about, triumphantly riding a white horse. And instead of a mellow hippy who turns a blind eye to any wrongdoing, they will encounter a sovereign King with a passion for righteousness, and a desire to vindicate those who have suffered and been martyred for his name.

Otherwise known as the King of Kings and Lord of Lords. All hail, King Jesus!

SON OF GOD AND SON OF MAN

· · · · · ·

And the high priest said to him, "I adjure you by the living God, tell
us if you are the Christ, the Son of God." Jesus said to him, "You have
said so. But I tell you, from now on you will see the Son of Man seated
at the right hand of Power and coming on the clouds of heaven." Then
the high priest tore his robes and said, "He has uttered blasphemy."
—Matthew 26:63–65

Jesus said he was both the Son of God and the Son of Man, and he
is. I don't know about you, but I spent a lot of my life confused as to
exactly what that means.

I always assumed he was basically stating what the creeds said about him.
To me, calling himself Son of God meant that he was the second person of
the Trinity, and calling himself Son of Man meant that he was as human as
you or me. So in the trial before the Sanhedrin that we have just read about,
I thought Jesus was saying that he was fully God and fully man.

But then I discovered some things that made me reconsider. I found that in the Old Testament, which Jesus knew extremely well, Israel was called God's firstborn son (Ex. 4:22–23; Jer. 31:20), and so was the king (2 Sam. 7:14; Ps. 89:26), but that this in no way suggested Israel or the king were divine. I found that another Jewish sect, from a similar period, used the phrase "son of God" to refer to the Messiah, not a divine figure.[1] I also found that, often in the gospels, "Son of God" and "Christ" were used together, like they are in this scene, as if they were saying virtually the same thing. Gradually, it became clear that when Matthew, Mark, and Luke talked about the Son of God, it had more to do with being the promised Messiah of Israel than it did with being God incarnate. There are lots of reasons to believe that Jesus saw himself as God, not least the way he talked about his relationship with his Father (using incredibly intimate language like Abba [Papa] and saying things like, "I and the Father are one"); but the title Son of God in itself is not one of them.

At the same time, though, I realized that "Son of Man" did not simply mean that Jesus was human. Although it could mean only that, it seemed to mean much more when Jesus used it of himself. In Daniel 7:13, we read about someone "like a son of man" approaching the Ancient of Days—that is, God—with the clouds of heaven, and sharing his throne, glory, and kingdom. I then noticed that when Jesus talked about himself as the Son of Man, he often made reference to this passage, suggesting that he thought about himself as that someone, the one who would approach God and share his dominion over all things: "For the Son of Man is going to come with his angels in the glory of his Father" (Matt. 16:27–28); "For as the lightning flashes and lights up the sky from one side to the other, so will the Son of Man be in his day" (Luke 17:24); "When the Son of Man comes in his glory, and all the angels with him, then he will sit on his glorious throne" (Matt. 25:31); "Then they will see the Son of Man coming in clouds with great power and glory" (Mark 13:26).

So in the Gospels, "Son of God" was used to mean the Christ, but "Son of Man" to mean the almost divine figure in Daniel 7 who shares the authority of the Ancient of Days. I realized I had got things upside down. It now looked as if calling himself the Son of Man was an even bigger claim, and certainly not a smaller one, than calling himself the Son of God. If anything, "Son of God" showed he was man, as the promised king of Israel, and "Son of Man" suggested he might be God.

The clincher is the trial scene in Matthew 26. The high priest had asked Jesus if he was the Son of God. From what we know about the high priest, this was almost certainly about being the Christ; devout Jews were very unlikely to be asking a Jewish prophet and would-be Messiah whether he was the second person of the Trinity. Jesus then answers that he is, on the high priest's own testimony (the phrase has the sense of "You've said it")—but that soon they will all see the Son of Man at the right hand of God, and coming on the clouds of heaven.

Quite apart from being yet another reference to Daniel 7, just think about this reply for a minute. It doesn't sound as if Jesus is downgrading, does it? It doesn't sound like they are asking if he is fully God, and he is saying, "Yes, but I am also fully man." It sounds like he is upgrading, dramatically. It sounds like a schoolboy who has just been secretly cast as the lead part in a Hollywood blockbuster—when the bullies ask him, "Did you come top of the class in drama?" he replies, "You said it; but from now on you will see me as Harry Potter, on billboards and film screens all over the country!" The high priest realizes the scandal of this claim, tears his robes, and announces that Jesus has committed blasphemy. Like Stephen a few months later, Jesus was condemned for blasphemy, not for referring to the Son of God, but the Son of Man.

You can see why. For someone to claim that he was the promised king of Israel was bad enough, but to say he was also the one who would share the throne with God himself and establish an everlasting kingdom was an outrage. But it was true. Far more true than the priests realized. Within a few years, those priests had died and gone, but the Son of God and Son of Man was seated at the right hand of the Ancient of Days: "And to him was given dominion and glory and a kingdom, that all peoples, nations and languages should serve him; his dominion is an everlasting dominion, which shall not pass away, and his kingdom one that shall not be destroyed" (Dan. 7:14).

Endnote
1. That is, the Qumran community (4Q174).

THE LORD IS THE SPIRIT

· · · · · ·

*Yes, to this day whenever Moses is read a veil lies over their hearts.
But when one turns to the Lord, the veil is removed. Now the Lord
is the Spirit, and where the Spirit of the Lord is, there is freedom.*
—*2 Corinthians 3:15–17*

The Holy Spirit is fully God. Nothing too controversial there. But while we may believe this, we don't often act like it in our worship, teaching, and practice. On the contrary, we are extraordinarily vague about him: The vast majority of our songs and hymns don't mention him; the same is often true of our books and sermons; and much of what he does— filling and empowering people, inspiring prophecy, giving various gifts like tongues and interpretation and healing—has frequently been shut out of the Western church. You cannot imagine any pagans in the period of the Acts (or in modern-day China, for that matter) mistaking the Trinity for the Father, Son, and Mary, as many Muslims do today. Nor would anyone who had met Paul be left wondering whether the Spirit's gifts were for every believer. The early church worshipped, knew, and experienced the Holy Spirit as fully God.

In large part, this was a theological belief about the nature of God. People listened to Jesus, reflected on the Scriptures, and saw that God was three in one, Father, Son, and Spirit:

"Now there are varieties of gifts, but the same Spirit; and there are varieties of service, but the same Lord; and there are varieties of activities, but the same God who empowers them all in everyone" (1 Cor. 12:4–6).

"The grace of the Lord Jesus Christ and the love of God and the fellowship of the Holy Spirit be with you all" (2 Cor. 13:14).

"According to the foreknowledge of God the Father, in the sanctification of the Spirit, for obedience to Jesus Christ and for sprinkling with his blood" (1 Peter 1:2).

Now, within this understanding of the Holy Spirit as God, Paul's phrase "Now the Lord is the Spirit" is very important. What does it mean? It could mean "Yahweh is the Spirit" (because the word for "Lord" is the word that translates "Yahweh" in the Old Testament), or it could mean "Jesus is the Spirit" (because Paul usually means Jesus when he talks about "the Lord"). The context, though, makes it likely that it means the first of these, not the second.

Paul has been making a long comparison between the glory of the New Covenant and the old. In these verses, he is saying that, just as Moses removed the physical veil from his face when he turned toward Yahweh in the tent of meeting, so believers today have their spiritual veil removed when they turn toward Yahweh in faith. Do you see? The analogy from Exodus, which he has been developing since verse 7, wouldn't work unless Paul was using the word Lord to mean Yahweh.

Furthermore, it is very unlikely that Paul, who sees the work of Jesus and the Spirit as clearly different, would teach that Jesus and the Spirit were the same. It is therefore very likely that he means "now Yahweh is the Spirit," or even "now the Spirit is Yahweh." This conviction, that the Spirit is fully God, is how Paul could say that to be lived in by the Spirit was to be God's temple (1 Cor. 3:16); it is also, incidentally, how Peter could say that to lie to the Spirit was to lie to God (Acts 5:1–10). The Spirit is God.

For Paul, the divine Holy Spirit was a theological conviction. But he was not just that. He was also an experienced reality, and you can see why. Imagine you were a first-century Jew, who had read and studied your Old Testament, and had seen Yahweh reveal himself through the Spirit, the Glory-cloud, the Law, the Word, and Wisdom. Imagine you had seen the Word and Wisdom perfectly embodied in the man Jesus of Nazareth, who had since been raised from the dead.

Now imagine it dawning on you that the Spirit (of power and prophecy), the Glory-cloud (with its dynamic manifestation of God's presence) and the Law (with its revelation of how to live a life pleasing to God) had been perfectly brought together in the Holy Spirit, and that he was living in each and every believer. Would you not be eager, enthusiastic, even expectant, that he would bring to your life the power, the prophecy, the presence of God, and the revelation of how to please him that you had been waiting for? Would you not, in fact, anticipate the Spirit to work miracles among you, bring regular prophetic revelation, cause the dynamic presence of God to be felt, and teach you how to live a holy life on a day-to-day basis?

This, if you read Romans, 1 and 2 Corinthians, Ephesians, and Colossians, is exactly what Paul expected, and exactly what he experienced. It was also, if you read Acts, exactly what pretty much everyone else experienced. If we see the Spirit as being present to inspire the Bible and not much else, then of course we will not worship, teach, and experience him as fully God like the early church did. But if we see him as the Spirit of promise, the power of God, the fulfillment of scriptures like Ezekiel 36 and Joel 2 and Jeremiah 31 and Isaiah 61, we will expect and experience the indwelling, guidance, baptism, and filling of the Holy Spirit of God.

Don't let us stop at theology. Let us continue into worshipping and experiencing the Lord, who is the Spirit.

# READ AND REFLECT

If you're not careful, it is easy to get fuzzy about the Holy Spirit. Read carefully through the following four passages (which are probably the clearest explanations of what the age of the Spirit would look like in the entire Old Testament), and identify what sorts of things the Holy Spirit does amongst his people. Then ask God to fill you again with his Spirit (Eph. 5:18)—and expect these sorts of things to happen in your life!

> The Spirit of Yahweh God is upon me, because Yahweh has anointed me to bring good news to the poor; he has sent me to bind up the brokenhearted, to proclaim liberty to the captives, and the opening of the prison to those who are bound; to proclaim the year of Yahweh's favor, and the day of vengeance of our God; to comfort all who mourn; to grant to those who mourn in Zion—to give them a beautiful headdress instead of ashes, the oil of gladness instead of mourning, the garment of praise instead of a faint spirit; that they may be called oaks of righteousness, the planting of Yahweh, that he may be glorified. (Isa. 61:1–3)

Behold, the days are coming, declares Yahweh, when I will make a new covenant with the house of Israel and the house of Judah, not like the covenant that I made with their fathers on the day when I took them by the hand to bring them out of the land of Egypt, my covenant that they broke, though I was their husband, declares Yahweh. But this is the covenant that I will make with the house of Israel after those days, declares Yahweh: I will put my law within them, and I will write it on their hearts. And I will be their God, and they shall be my people. And no longer shall each one teach his neighbor and each his brother, saying, "Know Yahweh," for they shall all know me, from the least of them to the greatest, declares Yahweh. For I will forgive their iniquity, and I will remember their sin no more. (Jer. 31:31–34)

Therefore say to the house of Israel, Thus says Yahweh God: It is not for your sake, O house of Israel, that I am about to act, but for the sake of my holy name, which you have profaned among the nations to which you came. And I will vindicate the holiness of my great name, which has been profaned among the nations, and which you have profaned among them. And the nations will know that I am Yahweh, declares Yahweh God, when through you I vindicate my holiness before their eyes. I will take you from the nations and gather you from all the countries and bring you into your own land. I will sprinkle clean water on you, and you shall be clean from all your uncleannesses, and from all your idols I will cleanse you. And I will give you a new heart, and a new spirit I will put within you. And I will remove the heart of stone from your flesh and give you a heart of flesh. And I will put my Spirit within you, and cause you to walk in my statutes and be careful to obey my rules. (Ezek. 36:22–27)

And it shall come to pass afterward, that I will pour out my Spirit on all flesh; your sons and your daughters shall prophesy, your old men shall dream dreams, and your young men shall see visions. Even on the male and female servants in those days I will pour out my Spirit. And I will show wonders in the heavens and on the earth, blood and fire and columns of smoke. The sun shall be turned to darkness, and the moon to blood, before the great and awesome day of Yahweh comes. And it shall come to pass that everyone who calls on the name of Yahweh shall be saved. For in Mount Zion and in Jerusalem there shall be those who escape, as Yahweh has said, and among the survivors shall be those whom Yahweh calls. (Joel 2:28–32)

THE HELPER

• • • • • •

Nevertheless, I tell you the truth: it is to your
advantage that I go away, for if I do not go away, the Helper
will not come to you. But if I go, I will send him to you.
—John 16:7

Some words have meanings so rich they cannot be properly translated.
The Hawaiian word "aloha" means hello, goodbye, welcome, and love,
all at once. The Hebrew *shalom* could be interpreted as peace, greet-
ings, farewell, or blessing. Sometimes, translating such a word can lose
so much of its meaning that it is better not to, or at least to list all of
its possible meanings when you do. A classic example is the word Jesus
uses to describe the Holy Spirit: *parakletos*.

There are almost as many translations of this word as there are
Bible versions. I have come across Helper, Advocate, Counselor,
Comforter, Encourager, and Friend, and some don't even translate it

at all, leaving it as Paraclete. Of course, the word is richer than can be brought across in any one translation, and it has nuances of all of these. For the moment we are going to stick with Helper, remembering that the word is really far deeper than that.

Whichever name we use, however, it should be very clear that the Spirit is a person. The church has often dropped the ball on this one; I am always amazed (and concerned!) by the number of people I know who refer to the Holy Spirit as an "it," rather than a "he." Perhaps this is because of the impersonal pictures Scripture uses, like wind and breath and fire; perhaps it is because we all know that fathers and sons are people, but the word "spirit" is a little bit vague in our normal usage. Whatever the reason, the truth remains that the Holy Spirit is most clearly a person who teaches (John 14:26), has opinions (Acts 15:28), distributes gifts (1 Cor. 12:11), intercedes (Rom. 8:26–27), and can be grieved (Eph. 4:30). If instead of calling him the Holy Spirit we called him the Friend or the Comforter, there would be no doubt about his personhood!

He is not just a person, though, but someone who gets so close to us that it beggars belief. Follow his activity through that marvelous chapter, Romans 8. As Helper, the Spirit sets us free, helps us set our minds on the things of God, and brings life to us (8:2–11). As Counselor, he is the one who knows all things advises us on how to make ordinary decisions, leading us according to his will, which proves that we are sons of God (8:12–14). As Comforter, the Holy Spirit comes alongside us in our trouble, reminds us that we are children of God, and helps us see that "the sufferings of this present time are not worth comparing to the glory that is to be revealed to us" (8:15–18). As

Advocate, he "helps us in our weakness. For we do not know what to pray for as we ought, but the Spirit himself intercedes for us" (8:26). These are activities of a person, but not just any person; they are the activity of Yahweh himself, by his holy and life-giving Spirit.

We get a glimpse in all this of why on earth Jesus said, "It is for your good that I go away." Of course it is for our good! Jesus taught the truth incessantly, but was still confronted by disciples who didn't understand him at all, and could not bear the teaching he would give; the Spirit, by living within them, guided them into all the truth. Jesus preached a gospel of repentance, but ended up rejected by the world; the Spirit convicted the world in regard to righteousness. Jesus was constrained by a physical body that meant he could only be in one place at once; the Spirit was able to empower witnesses in Jerusalem, Judea, Samaria, and to the utmost ends of the earth, and he still does. Were Jesus the man still walking the earth, I could expect to get one billionth of his time, and he would show up in my church about once every 20,000 years. The Helper, by contrast, lives in me twenty-four hours a day, helps me in my weakness, prays for me, reveals truth to me, and comes with me to every church service and car service I ever go to.

This is why Pentecost was such a big deal. God, whose house had always been made of cloth or stone, was taking up residence in people, and this showed he had forgiven their sins. The prophets had looked forward to a time when God's Spirit would be poured out on people as a sign of his forgiveness; the apostles could see it happening in front of them. The prophets predicted that the Spirit would be given to all types of people, as a sign that they too had been accepted into the people of God; the apostles realized that this is exactly what had just happened. The Spirit of God was truly coming to dwell in people, and this in itself was a guarantee that those people would have an eternal inheritance. Yahweh had kept his covenant, left the Temple, upped sticks, and moved into people.

So history changed. With that decision—to ascend into heaven and send the Helper in his place—Jesus set in motion an incredible plan, to see people from all sorts of different nations and languages born again, made holy, and united together. And the agent of this plan was, as it could only ever have been, the most gloriously effective Helper, Advocate, Counselor, Comforter, Encourager, and Friend that the world has ever seen. The Holy Spirit of God.

• • • • • •

EXPLORATION IV
The Attributes of God

• • • • • •

THE KNOWLEDGE OF GOD

• • • • • •

Oh, the depth of the riches and wisdom and knowledge of God! How
unsearchable are his judgments and how inscrutable his ways! "For who
has known the mind of the Lord, or who has been his counselor?"
—Romans 11:33–34

In 2005, the United States spent nearly two trillion dollars on over-
coming ignorance. We call it the education budget, but that's what it
is. Fifteen cents out of every American dollar was spent on informing people of things they didn't know before: teaching children to
read, instructing teenagers on history and literature, helping research-
ers find out things. We are born ignorant, and much of our lifetime
is spent trying to overcome it. Even when we have learned how to
move, speak, read, and write, our lives are filled with ignorance—of
the consequences of our behavior, of how to be a good parent, of other
cultures and languages, of what the stock market will do next week.

Just think how many people have said, "If only I'd known then what I know now ..."

God does not have this problem. As Psalm 147:5 puts it, "His understanding is beyond measure." God has never needed to go to school. There are no jobs for which he is not qualified. He never gets the wrong end of the stick or makes a social blunder. He has never lost his car keys, forgotten somebody's name, gotten his words wrong, or worried about what will happen tomorrow. Confusion, surprise, anxiety, and frustration—all of them part of our daily experience—are just not things that God has ever undergone. His knowledge is, quite simply, infinite.

Theologians call this "omniscience," which means "being all-knowing." In Paul's language, God's knowledge is so deep that it cannot be searched out or scrutinized by us. It is no coincidence that this song of praise comes at the end of three very densely argued chapters about God's sovereign choice and eternal plan. In fact, the doxology of Romans 11 underpins the theology of Romans 9. Paul wants us to know that ultimately, we are in no position to argue the toss with God, so deep and profound are his decisions. Verse 34 effectively asks: Who has ever known what God is thinking? Who could advise God on the best plan of action? He knows *everything*.

I love the way John Piper expresses the knowledge of God in Romans 11:

> Paul says that God's knowledge is unfathomably deep. He knows all recorded facts—all the facts stored in all the computers and all the books in all the libraries in the

world. But vastly more than that, he knows all events at the macro level—all that happens on earth and in the atmosphere and in all the farthest reaches of space in every galaxy and star and planet. And all events at the micro level—all that happens in molecules and atoms and electrons and protons and neutrons and quarks. He knows all their movements and every location and every condition of every particle of the universe at every nanosecond of time … When one event happens, he not only sees it, but he sees the eternal chain of effects that flow from it and from all the billions of events that are unleashed by every other event. He knows all this without the slightest strain on his mind. That is what it means to be God.[1]

So God knows all things in the physical universe. But reflect for a moment on three other types of things that God knows.

First, he knows all thoughts. Knowing things in the physical world is impressive, but we can perhaps understand how that might be possible. For God to know our thoughts, however, is impossible to grasp. It means that nothing—not even what goes on in your brain—is beyond God's sight. No wonder, after saying to God, "You discern my thoughts from afar," David concludes, "such knowledge is too wonderful for me; it is high; I cannot attain it" (Ps. 139:2–6).

Second, he knows even things that are not done. Stephen Charnock, the great Puritan preacher, points out:

This the Scripture gives us some account of: God knows things that are not, "for he calls things that are not as if they were" (Romans 4:17) … he knew that the inhabitants of Keilah would betray David to Saul if he remained in that place (1 Samuel 23:11); *he knew what they would do upon that occasion, though it was never done.*[2]

So God not only knows all things that happen, but he also knows all things which would have happened under different circumstances. He knows all possible outcomes from every situation.

Third, God knows all future events. We could get into a big debate about this, but put simply: If you look through the Bible, you will find dozens of things—the names of children, the fates of nations, and the decisions of unbelievers, for instance—predicted with total accuracy by Almighty God. This is a great source of comfort for us as ignorant, confused, anxious people!

God knows all past, present, and future events, all thoughts and all possibilities. Oh, the depth of the riches and the wisdom and the knowledge of God!

Endnotes
1. *John Piper, speaking at Bethlehem Baptist Church, Minneapolis, in March 2004.*
2. *Stephen Charnock,* The Existence and Attributes of God *(Grand Rapids, MI: Baker, 2000), 1: 417, italics added.*

 PAUSE AND PRAY

The fact that God knows everything should be an enormous comfort to us, and a huge provocation to pray to him and cast all our anxieties upon him (1 Peter 5:6–7). In Psalm 139, David gives an example of how to ground our prayers in the all-encompassing knowledge of God. You might like to pray through it with him, and with the millions who have used it through the centuries.

O Yahweh, you have searched me and known me! You know when I sit down and when I rise up; you discern my thoughts from afar. You search out my path and my lying down and are acquainted with all my ways. Even before a word is on my tongue, behold, O Yahweh, you know it altogether. You hem me in, behind and before, and lay your hand upon me. Such knowledge is too wonderful for me; it is high; I cannot attain it.

Where shall I go from your Spirit? Or where shall I flee from your presence? If I ascend to heaven, you are there! If I make my bed in Sheol, you are there! If I take the wings of the morning and dwell in the uttermost parts of the sea, even there your hand shall lead me, and your right hand shall hold me. If I say, "Surely the darkness shall cover me, and the light about me be night," even the darkness is not dark to you; the night is bright as the day, for darkness is as light with you.

For you formed my inward parts; you knitted me together in my mother's womb. I praise you, for I am fearfully and wonderfully made. Wonderful are your works; my soul knows it very well. My frame was not hidden from you, when I was being made in secret, intricately woven in the depths of the earth. Your eyes saw my unformed substance; in your book were written, every one of them, the days that were formed for me, when as yet there was none of them. How precious to me are your thoughts, O God! How vast is the sum of them! If I would count them, they are more than the sand. I awake, and I am still with you.

Oh that you would slay the wicked, O God! O men of blood, depart from me! They speak against you with malicious intent; your enemies take your name in vain! Do I not hate those who hate you, O Yahweh? And do I not loathe those who rise up against you? I hate them with complete hatred; I count them my enemies. Search me, O God, and know my heart! Try me and know my thoughts! And see if there be any grievous way in me, and lead me in the way everlasting!

THE GREATNESS OF YAHWEH

• • • • • •

*Who has measured the waters in the hollow of his hand and marked
off the heavens with a span, enclosed the dust of the earth in a measure
and weighed the mountains in scales and the hills in a balance? Who
has measured the Spirit of Yahweh, or what man shows him counsel?*
—Isaiah 40:12–13

We need to be slapped in the face with the greatness of Yahweh.
Human problems will never be solved by economics, or politics, or
science, or self-help, but only by a renewed understanding of the
wonder and glory and majesty of Almighty God. I remember the
first time I read Tozer's *The Knowledge of the Holy,* and this truth
hit me right between the eyes: "It is my opinion that the Christian
conception of God … is so decadent as to be utterly beneath the
dignity of the Most High God and actually to constitute for pro-
fessed believers something amounting to a moral calamity … The

essence of idolatry is the entertainment of thoughts about God that are unworthy of Him."[1]

Sin results from knowing God but not responding appropriately to his greatness (Rom. 1:21). So every person suffers from a sickness for which an understanding of the greatness of God is the only medicine.

If we agree with Tozer's assessment of our problem, and I do, then we need Isaiah 40. We need it because it presents a God so great that our response to him can only be worship and amazement. Isaiah deliberately presents a series of rhetorical questions designed to bring out the sheer bigness of God, by taking massive earthly things—the seas, the skies, the land, and the mountains—and making them seem almost ridiculously small in comparison to God. Let's look at them one at a time.

The first question is, "Who has measured the waters in the hollow of his hand?" If you cup your hand now, you will see how small the hollow of your hand is. Depending on your size, you will be able to hold up to about one hundred milliliters of water in it. Now consider: How big would you have to be to hold all the world's water in the hollow of your hand? Every day, the world experiences forty-five thousand thunderstorms. If you look at the earth from space, you can see them, flashing around all over the place. Each thundercloud in each one of these thunderstorms contains, on average, one hundred thousand tons of water. And that's just the clouds. The four Great Lakes, if they were poured out over the continental United States, would cover the whole country, two and a half yards deep. The oceans, more dramatically, contain around 328 million *cubic miles* of water. And Isaiah pictures Yahweh as measuring all of them in the hollow of his hand.

Now, instead of cupping your hand, stretch it out to form a hand-span. My handspan is about the same size as a banana. God's is big enough to "mark off the heavens." Our minds are simply unable to grasp this, because the heavens are so big, but a couple of illustrations may help. If the 93 million miles from here to the sun were represented by the thickness of one piece of paper, it would take a stack 25 yards high to reach from earth to the *nearest* star. And there are so many stars that if you were to count the ones in our galaxy alone, at the rate of three every second, 24 hours a day, it would take you a millennium. Counting all the stars in the universe would take slightly longer: one hundred trillion years. Yet Yahweh is so great that his handspan is easily big enough to mark off all of them.

God also encloses the dust of the earth in a measure, and weighs the mountains and the hills. We are probably a bit more able to cope with this mentally, but it is still mind-bending. Imagine fitting the Sahara desert into your measuring jug, or sizing up the Himalayas on your bathroom scales! Even today, climbing Mount Everest is a pinnacle of human achievement; it is so high and so hostile that a hundred and eighty people have died trying, and most of us have no way of getting hold of how big it actually is. Yet Yahweh "weighs the mountains."

So we have a God who is so great that the very biggest things we know about—the earth, the mountains, the oceans, and the skies themselves—are small enough to fit in his hands and be weighed in his balances. Who, Isaiah therefore asks, can fathom the Spirit of Yahweh, or dare to advise God?

We need revelation of the greatness of this God. In a world where there are no shortages of people lining up to advise God on how to do his job, reflecting on the great Yahweh described in Isaiah 40 will burst our bubbles, and bring us from our high horses to our knees. If we have a picture of Yahweh's greatness in our souls, we will not argue with him or apologize for him, but will wonder at him and worship him. How great is our God!

Endnote
1. A. W. Tozer, The Knowledge of the Holy *(New York: HarperOne, 1998; Milton Keynes: Authentic, 2005), 3.*

THE JUSTICE OF YAHWEH

• • • • • •

O Yahweh, you hear the desire of the afflicted; you will strengthen their
heart; you will incline your ear to do justice to the fatherless and the
oppressed, so that man who is of the earth may strike terror no more.
—Psalm 10:17–18

In April 1994, an untold number of Rwandans were hacked to death
with machetes. Men on their way to work were seized and chopped
to pieces. Women were dragged from their homes and murdered in
front of their families. Terrified children, sometimes taking refuge
in churches, were clubbed to death in vast numbers. In a stadium in
Kibuye, the mob of attackers was so exhausted after a day of murder-
ing their neighbors that they sealed the stadium, went home for a rest,
and returned the next day to finish the job. Before the West had done
anything to stop it, the Tutsi body count had reached hundreds of
thousands.

Most of us are fairly apathetic about justice. The chances are, when we first heard about the events I've just described, we didn't have a particularly strong reaction. We listened to the news, which made things seem more distant by using words like "tribal" and "genocide," then we made a face of mild disgust, and carried on with the rest of the day. We have the same reaction every time we read a newspaper. It's not a bad thing, actually, since it helps us cope with normal life in a world polluted by sin. But we are so corrupted by sin—so used to injustices like lying and fornicating and gossip and greed—that in order for us to get a true perspective of the outrage and fury of Yahweh when injustice occurs, it helps us to be shocked into a feeling of outrage and fury ourselves.

The alternative is to read the Psalms and the prophets. They describe a God who is so passionate about justice, and so angry about injustice, that you want to hide from him. The Bible doesn't pretend that bad things never happen. All our graphic modern injustices are in Scripture: bonded child labor (Job 24:9), rape (Judg. 19:22–26), killing pregnant women (Amos 1:13), ethnic cleansing (Est. 3:13), and so on. What the Bible does, though, is to explain that even through these terrible evils, there is hope of justice, because of the character of Yahweh. Justice is when God works out what belongs to whom, and makes sure that they get it.[1]

Take Psalm 10. In just a few verses, it mentions colossal injustices like deceit, crushing the helpless, seizing the poor, and murder (in terms strikingly similar to the Rwandan genocide), and explains why such things take place:

"He sits in ambush in the villages; in hiding places he murders the innocent … He says in his heart, 'God has forgotten, he has hidden his face, he will never see it'" (8–11).

But then comes the hope of justice: "But you do see" (v. 14). For all that man behaves as if he will never get caught, God sees. One of three things causes injustice: impotence (a lack of power to do anything about it); ignorance (a lack of awareness of evil); and impassivity (a lack of compassion). In verses 16–18, we see that Yahweh suffers from none of these problems, with absolute power ("Yahweh is king for ever and ever"), knowledge ("you hear the desire of the afflicted"), and compassion ("you will incline your ear to do justice to the fatherless and the oppressed"). The net result is that man can no longer "strike terror."

Today, we may rightly wonder how this works, since enormous injustices continue to take place. Doesn't man, who is of the earth, continue to strike terror? Isn't he getting away with it? Well, several things need to be said here. First, we need an eternal perspective. If we have read passages like James 5:1–6 properly, we will see that the rapist or murderer has no more gotten away with it than the casino thief running toward the door with an armful of cash, before being seized by an army of security guards—we just need to wind the story forward a bit. Second, God's heart for the victims is broken infinitely more than ours, because he can hear their cries all at once. We hear about child prostitution and then flick over to the film channel, but Yahweh experiences the pain and suffering of every rape victim and slave and orphan, and experiences them simultaneously.

Third, God's main way of bringing justice to the earth is through his people, so if injustice is rampant, it is because the church isn't doing anything. This is the logic of the book of Amos: It is Israel, not God, who is rebuked because there is no justice (Amos 2:6–8). Gary Haugen, founder of the human rights group International Justice Mission is very helpful here:

> No thoughtful Christian would say, "Sure Jesus wants his gospel preached, the hungry fed, the sick healed, and the naked clothed, but that doesn't have anything to do with me." And yet many of us have been content to praise God as the God of justice, to extol his compassion for the weak and voiceless and to declare his promises to "rescue the life of the needy from the hands of the wicked"—all the while harboring a suspicion that God generally accomplishes these miracles with mysterious winds or vague, magical forces of history … we may be tempted to shake our fist at God, demanding to know why he's not harder at work … Like the Israelites we often weary God with our words, saying, "Where is the God of justice?" (Mal. 2:17).[2]

Yahweh is outraged at injustice, a day of reckoning is coming, and he has given his people a mandate to stop it. So we should rejoice in, and live for, the God of justice—so that man, who is of the earth, may strike terror no more.

Endnotes
1. *This statement is attributed to the Old Testament scholar Walter Brueggemann.*
2. *Gary A. Haugen,* Good News About Injustice *(Downers Grove, IL: InterVarsity, 2002; Leicester: IVP, 1999), 99.*

THE MERCY OF YAHWEH

· · · · · ·

Yahweh passed before him and proclaimed, "Yahweh, Yahweh, a God merciful and gracious, slow to anger, and abounding in steadfast love and faithfulness, keeping steadfast love for thousands, forgiving iniquity and transgression and sin, but who will by no means clear the guilty, visiting the iniquity of the fathers on the children and the children's children, to the third and the fourth generation."
—Exodus 34:6–7

Mercy and justice seem to stand in tension. Someone who is guilty, we reckon, can either be met with justice (being punished) or mercy (being let off). Justice involves acting without mercy; mercy involves momentarily suspending justice. So, we assume, you can't be both merciful and just at the same time.

If this is true, then no one has told Yahweh. Time and again through Scripture, we find mercy and justice together; not played

240

off against one another, or even mentioned incidentally in the same sentence, but deliberately paired, to give a balanced view of God and his law:

> Therefore Yahweh waits to be *gracious* to you, and therefore he exalts himself to show *mercy* to you. For Yahweh is a God of <u>justice</u>; blessed are all those who wait for him. (Isa. 30:18)

> I will betroth you to me in <u>righteousness</u> and in <u>justice</u>, in *steadfast love* and in *mercy*. (Hos. 2:19)

> You ... have neglected the weightier matters of the law: <u>justice</u> and *mercy* and faithfulness. (Matt. 23:23)

> He has showed you, O man, what is good. And what does Yahweh require of you? To <u>act justly</u>, and to *love mercy*, and to walk humbly with your God. (Mic. 6:8 NIV)

Much as we would like to, we cannot wriggle out of this by saying that God is just sometimes and merciful sometimes. The quotation from Isaiah teaches us that Yahweh shows mercy *because* he is a God of justice. Moreover, if you look at the context of the verse we started with, you will find that this proclamation of mercy and justice is part of the revelation to Moses of Yahweh's name. Both mercy ("forgiving iniquity") and justice ("by no means clearing the guilty"), as much as they seem opposites here, are eternally part of his character. So if we see a contradiction between the two, we have misunderstood something.

I think the misunderstanding is this: We think Yahweh shows mercy to the guilty by suspending his justice. He doesn't. He shows mercy to the guilty by carrying out his justice on something or someone else. Put another way, mercy is not a just punishment's *disappearance*, but its *transfer*. If I get caught speeding, and the judge lets me off my fine, that is mercy at the expense of justice. It would be kind to me, but it would make a mockery of the speeding laws, and would ultimately undermine the authority of the judge himself. To show justice, the judge would have to ensure my fine was paid—so showing mercy to me would mean getting it paid by someone else. This, of course, is exactly what God does.

Look at the Old Testament sacrifices. Because of God's justice, Israel's sin had two consequences: death and separation from God. But because of his mercy, a sacrificial system was set up that meant animals, rather than people, could face these consequences. Thus, on the Day of Atonement described in Leviticus 16, one goat would be sacrificed (death), and the other would be sent out of the camp into the wilderness (separation from God). These animals allowed both God's mercy and his justice to be shown to the Israelites at the same time, ensuring that he did not "clear the guilty" (by overlooking their sin), but that he still "forgave iniquity" (by meting out his justice on something else). Wonderfully, mercy was so central to the whole system that the lid of the ark of the covenant itself, the centerpiece of the tabernacle and the place where Yahweh lived, was called the "mercy seat."

This system, though, was just a shadow of what was to come. The most definitive demonstration of God's mercy, the cross of Jesus Christ, was also the most powerful statement of his justice. One passage, which we did not list earlier, mixes mercy and justice more gloriously than any other:

> For all have sinned and fall short of the glory of God, being justified by his *grace* as a *gift*, through the redemption in Christ Jesus, whom God put forward as a *mercy seat* through faith in his blood. This was to show his righteousness, because in the *forbearance* of God he had passed over former sins; it was to show his righteousness at the present time, so that he might be just and *the justifier* of whoever has faith in Jesus. (Rom. 3:23–26, author's translation)

Do you see? The sacrifice of Christ demonstrated God's justice, but in doing so it made mercy available! Jesus, our sacrificial goat and our scapegoat, the one who experienced both death and separation from God on our behalf, was given as the mercy seat we need, in order to show God's righteousness.

Yahweh, Yahweh, a God merciful and gracious!

READ AND REFLECT

Mercy is not just a New Testament idea. In Psalm 103, regarded by many as the most complete and wonderful Psalm in the Bible, we have a stunning exposition of the mercy of God—particularly in his forgiveness of sins—and yet this Psalm was written a thousand years before the cross! Meditate on each line as you read through it, and see how much you can commit to memory.

Bless Yahweh, O my soul, and all that is within me, bless his holy name! Bless Yahweh, O my soul, and forget not all his benefits, who forgives all your iniquity, who heals all your diseases, who redeems your life from the pit, who crowns you with steadfast love and mercy, who satisfies you with good so that your youth is renewed like the eagle's.

Yahweh works righteousness and justice for all who are oppressed. He made known his ways to Moses, his acts to the people of Israel. Yahweh is merciful and gracious, slow to anger and abounding in steadfast love. He will not always chide, nor will he keep his anger forever. He does not deal with us according to our sins, nor repay us according to our iniquities.

For as high as the heavens are above the earth, so great is his steadfast love toward those who fear him; as far as the east is from the west, so far does he remove our transgressions from us. As a father shows compassion to his children, so Yahweh shows compassion to those who fear him. For he knows our frame; he remembers that we are dust.

As for man, his days are like grass; he flourishes like a flower of the field; for the wind passes over it, and it is gone, and its place knows it no more. But the steadfast love of Yahweh is from everlasting to everlasting on those who fear him, and his righteousness to children's children, to those who keep his covenant and remember to do his commandments. Yahweh has established his throne in the heavens, and his kingdom rules over all.

Bless Yahweh, O you his angels, you mighty ones who do his word, obeying the voice of his word! Bless Yahweh, all his hosts, his ministers, who do his will! Bless Yahweh, all his works, in all places of his dominion. Bless Yahweh, O my soul!

THE WISDOM OF YAHWEH

• • • • • •

O Yahweh, how manifold are your works! In wisdom have
you made them all; the earth is full of your creatures. Here
is the sea, great and wide, which teems with creatures innu-
merable, living things both small and great.
—Psalm 104:24–25

The world is a display case of the wisdom of Yahweh. The earth and
heavens were established in the first place by his wisdom (Jer. 51:15),
the gospel is a demonstration of how wise God is (1 Cor. 1:24), and the
centerpiece of God's story, the church, exists to make known "the mul-
tifold wisdom of God" (Eph. 3:10). Yet nothing in the universe makes
Yahweh's wisdom more blatant to me than the "manifold works" and
"innumerable creatures" that Psalm 104 is talking about.

Creatures clearly show the foolishness of humankind; humankind,
whose most popular theory about the formation of life—complete

chance—has been reckoned by a professor of biophysics at Yale to have a probability of 1 in $10^{340,000,000}$ (or the chance of enough people to fill the solar system, all blindfolded, solving a Rubik's Cube simultaneously).[1] More than that, however, the existence of even one of God's creatures is enough to persuade us of the astonishing wisdom of God. As we consider a few of them, ask yourself: How wise would you have to be to create one?

The guillemot bird has to lay eggs high up on rocky crags, to avoid predators. So as to avoid them being blown over the cliffs, she lays her eggs spinning, which hugely increases their chance of survival. Quite apart from wondering about the gymnastics of that process, knowing this makes me wonder how on earth she learnt to do that, unless a God of manifold wisdom taught her. The idea of evolution by chance, or even creation by a less-than-wise God, disappears out of the window when you look at a guillemot bird laying her eggs.

One of the most unlikely things to have evolved by chance is the bombardier beetle. This bizarre animal has a very unusual defense mechanism. It has tubes in its tail that store two different chemicals, and these chemicals, when mixed together, cause an explosion. It also has a third substance, an inhibitor, which prevents any explosion from taking place until the chemicals enter a chamber in its rear; at this point an enzyme is added and an explosion takes place, firing a 212-degree jet out of its backside at its enemies, and propelling itself several yards away. Random chance or unintelligent design would never have produced a bombardier beetle—just a trail of attempts (each blown to smithereens!).[2] For the wisdom of Yahweh, however, it is no trouble.

A more everyday creature, the honeybee, communicates to its

worker bees the whereabouts of the pollen it has found. That in itself is remarkable. But its method almost beggars belief: It performs a circular dance, inside the hive, to describe the direction in which they should travel, and adjusts its motion to take windspeed into account, so that the worker bees do not get blown off course as they fly. That is not bad work for a creature whose brain is not much larger than a full stop. "O Yahweh, how manifold are your works! In wisdom have you made them all."

Or take water. You may have learned in chemistry that water is the only substance in the world that is lighter as a solid than as a liquid, which is why ice floats, rather than sinks. This may seem unimportant, but just think: If the solid form (ice) sank in the liquid form (water), as every other substance does, the icebergs would sink to the seabed rather than float toward the equator to be melted, and the oceans would freeze from the bottom up. Even common happenings on the planet are an astonishing witness to the wisdom of Yahweh.

We could go on, as the psalmist knows: "Here is the sea, great and wide, which teems with creatures innumerable." The electric eel fires a 300-volt blast of electricity to stun its prey. The black-fly larva, which lives in fast-flowing river currents, attaches itself to the riverbed with a hook, and also has a long, retractable silken line stretching out of its mouth with which to pull itself back onto the rock if it loses its grip. Every one of the billions of snowflakes that fall each year is different. Migratory birds travel thousands of miles across featureless oceans to exactly the same place each year. And so on.

But as impressive as all of these things are, they are not intended to be clever in themselves. All things in creation, from the guillemot to the gospel, act as continual reminders—like pop-up boxes on the Internet forever jumping out at you—that Yahweh is wise. As Paul, signing off perhaps the greatest letter ever written, exclaimed:

"To the only wise God be glory forevermore through Jesus Christ! Amen" (Rom. 16:27).

Endnotes

1. Harold J. Morowitz, Energy Flow in Biology *(New York: Academic, 1968), 99; the analogy is from Sir Fred Hoyle, former professor of astronomy at Cambridge University. So improbable is the chance formation of life on earth that Francis Crick, the discoverer of the structure of DNA and an atheist, had a bizarre theory: "Life on earth may have begun when aliens from another planet sent a rocket ship containing spores to seed the earth" (Francis Crick,* Life Itself: Its Origin and Nature *[New York: Simon and Schuster, 1981]). Some people will believe anything rather than believe in the wisdom of God.*

2. Pushed on this issue in an interview with Jonathan Miller, Richard Dawkins, perhaps the world's most high-profile atheist, made the remarkable admission: "Natural selection … well, I suppose that is a sort of matter of faith on my part since the theory is so coherent, and so powerful" (on BBC2's The Final Hour, *November 14, 2005, 7:00 p.m.). In the interview, the debate was over the development of a bird's wing.*

Yahweh Is My Strength
and My Song

• • • • • •

Then Moses and the people of Israel sang this song to Yahweh, say-
ing, "I will sing to Yahweh, for he has triumphed gloriously; the
horse and his rider he has thrown into the sea. Yahweh is my strength
and my song, and he has become my salvation; this is my God,
and I will praise him, my father's God, and I will exalt him."
—Exodus 15:1–2

Strength and song don't often go together. Many cultures, ours
included, seem to have divided the two: physically impressive strength,
a stereotypically masculine pursuit, represented by sporting competition, military might, and a tendency for action, versus emotionally
expressive song, which is more stereotypically feminine, and shows
itself through art, music, creativity, and a tendency for reflection. Little
boys who show traits of the latter may have it bullied out of them; little

girls who look like the former are labeled tomboys and regarded as needing to grow out of it. And you can almost always divide a classroom of teenagers into sporty ones and artsy ones.

This separation is not found in God. In fact, he is the ultimate example of both. Yahweh's strength, of course, is one of his most striking attributes—Scripture is full of his mighty conquests on behalf of his people, and his great power to raise up nations and crush them. He is a warrior God, the kind of person you would not want to meet on a dark night, a God of strength. Yet what a God of song! Yahweh created the world to the backdrop of explosive singing (Job 38:7), ended his last meal with his friends with a hymn (Mark 14:26), and will bring history to its climax with the loudest and most beautiful songs anyone has ever heard (Rev. 19). Yahweh's song is not effeminate, nor is his strength chauvinistic; both are glorious, and both come wonderfully together. (This should perhaps make us wary of gender-stereotyping people made in his image. The courage of the very feminine Esther, and the artistry of the very masculine David, should help us debunk some cultural prejudices.)

Look at the way strength (here underlined) and song (in italics) are united in Zephaniah 3:14–17:

> *Sing aloud, O daughter of Zion*; shout, O Israel! *Rejoice and exult with all your heart, O daughter of Jerusalem*! Yahweh has taken away the judgments against you; <u>he has cleared away your enemies</u>. The King of Israel, Yahweh, is in your midst; <u>you shall never again fear evil</u>. On that day it shall be said to Jerusalem: "<u>Fear not</u>, O Zion; <u>let not your hands</u>

grow weak. Yahweh your God is in your midst, <u>a mighty one who will save</u>; he will *rejoice over you with gladness*; he will quiet you by his love; *he will exult over you with loud singing.*"

We could stop there, and simply reflect on what it would be like to hear the "loud singing" of Yahweh. But there is more. It is not just that Yahweh is both a strong and a singing God. It is that Moses and the people of Israel, in Exodus 15:2, were able to declare that "Yahweh is *my* strength and *my* song."

It is fairly easy to see why they would sing, "Yahweh is my strength." Israel had just been rescued from Egypt in dramatic fashion, with the Red Sea parted in front of them, and then closed behind them to kill the chasing armies. The strength of God was not in question. However, they did not let their understanding of him stop there, affirming also that "Yahweh is my song." In other words, they were not content for God to be recognized merely as their provider of power. They wanted to acknowledge him as their source of joy as well. This is what the people of God do all through Scripture, whether in success or in suffering.

Here in Exodus, Yahweh is their strength and their song in success. The people who live down your road, whatever their religion, may claim strength from their beliefs when things have gone well, but there is no song. There is no personalized and emotional response of gratitude to anyone for what has happened, no equivalent to the song of Moses or of Miriam. As the apologist Michael Ramsden puts it, the reason people are unhappy in the world today is not because they have nothing to be grateful for, but because they have no one to be grateful to. Israel, on the other hand, knew exactly who to praise for their deliverance.

Singing is even rarer in suffering. If you don't believe that suffering will eventually end (Rev. 21:4), or that it will build your character in the meantime (James 1:2–3), or that it is earning you eternal reward (2 Cor. 4:17), then you have nothing to sing about—strength (the "grin and bear it" philosophy) is the best you can hope for. If you do, however, then you can sing with true joy, like Paul and Silas did in the Philippian jail (Acts 16:25). Remember, it was suffering slaves on the plantations, singing about the joys of God and an eternity with him, that laid the musical foundation for blues, jazz, gospel, and almost all modern rock music. They understood, like generations before them, that Yahweh was not just their strength, but also their song.

As the people of God today, we must not let this go. We must not reduce Yahweh to a means of getting through tough situations without celebrating him in the process. We must not just enjoy our triumphs, but give exuberant worship to him who worked them. We must enjoy Yahweh at all costs: our power and our praise, our might and our music, our deliverance and our delight. Our strength and our song.

THE WRATH OF YAHWEH

• • • • • •

Yahweh is a jealous and avenging God; Yahweh is avenging and
wrathful; Yahweh takes vengeance on his adversaries and keeps
wrath for his enemies. Yahweh is slow to anger and great in power,
and Yahweh will by no means clear the guilty. His way is in whirl-
wind and storm, and the clouds are the dust of his feet.
—Nahum 1:2–3

If we could choose which attribute of God we could remove, just like
that, I think most of us would choose his wrath. No one likes it. The
idea of Yahweh being "avenging and wrathful" and "keeping wrath for his
enemies" strikes us as medieval, nasty, and cruel, and it is often a source
of embarrassment in conversation with unbelievers. How very unmodern,
how unpleasant, to have a God who not only gets angry sometimes, but
actually lists being "wrathful" as one of his characteristics. So, dismayed
by the theology of Nahum, we hurriedly flick forward to a lovely letter

like Romans (only to find chapters 1–3 and 9), or to find out what that nice man from Nazareth had to say about things (as long as you ignore the Sermon on the Mount, many of the parables, and nearly everything he said in Jerusalem). To our horror, we discover that the wrath of God is everywhere. Clearly, Scripture is not as bothered by it as we are.

Yahweh is wrathful. He is angry about sin, and the terrible damage it has done to his creation. Every transgression of ours is an act of idolatry (putting something else, usually ourselves, before God); of adultery (responding to his commitment and love by rejecting him); and of sacrilege (living as if his holiness did not matter, and falling desperately short of his standard); and all of these things rightly result in his wrath toward us. In our blindness, though, we often regard the wrath of Yahweh as not worthy of him. I think there are three main causes of this misunderstanding.

The relationship between the old and new covenants is one of them. People with a superficial view of the Bible sometimes think that Yahweh was wrathful and jealous for his people in the Old Testament, but that with Jesus, those things subsided. Quite apart from the fact that Yahweh never changes (and the fact that the New Testament talks much more severely about many sins than the Old), this betrays a total failure to grasp why Jesus died. Jesus' death on the cross did not say, "It's all OK, because God is not angry with sin anymore." It said, "God is incredibly angry with sin, so angry that this is the only way to save you." Jesus did not tell people the building was not on fire, but reminded them that it was—and then proclaimed that he was the only Emergency Exit. That's why God's love, God's wrath, and Jesus' death are grouped together in the New Testament:

"God shows his *love* for us in that while we were still sinners, *Christ died* for us. Since, therefore, we have now been justified by his *blood*, much more shall we be saved by him from the *wrath* of God" (Rom. 5:8–9).

"[We] were by nature *children of wrath*, like the rest of mankind. But God, being rich in mercy, *because of the great love with which he loved us*, even when we were dead in our trespasses, made us alive" (Eph. 2:3–5).

"He is clothed in *a robe dipped in blood*, and the name by which he is called is The Word of God … He will tread *the winepress of the fury of the wrath of God the Almighty*" (Rev. 19:13–15).

The second misunderstanding is that God's wrath is somehow like ours—petty outbursts, driven by wounded pride or self-indulgence, divine toddler tantrums that result in pain and regret on all sides. If so, then the passage in Nahum we started with should put an end to it. Just after announcing God's vengeful wrath three times over, the prophet reminds his listeners of something God revealed to Moses on Mount Sinai: "Yahweh is slow to anger." God does not have mood swings, flying off the handle at the end of a bad day. His wrath is always measured, always appropriate, and always righteous, and this makes all the difference.

The third source of confusion is probably the biggest one: the idea that wrath and love are opposites. It is quite amazing how many people say things like "a loving God wouldn't do that" or "I believe God is love, not wrath," as if love and wrath were contradictory. But in response to genuine evil, the opposite of wrath is not love, but indifference. In John Grisham's novel *A Time to Kill,* an Afro-Caribbean father discovers his little girl has been raped by two white men, and in his wrath he shoots them; the story is powerful because, as readers, we know that vigilante justice is wrong and yet somehow feel that his wrath was the appropriate response to the crime. If we go around the Holocaust Museum and do not feel outraged that it happened, we are not loving, but apathetic. Similarly, a man who was not angry that his wife had been having an affair would not thereby demonstrate how much he loved her, but how little. So it is with God.

We need to respond to these misunderstandings with truth. The wrath of Yahweh is real and righteous and scary. Flying off the handle is completely beneath the Most High God, but so is indifference to the horror of sin, and we need to adjust our thinking to cope with this. The fact is, whether we like the idea of God's wrath or not, we will all one day witness it for ourselves. As John saw:

"Then the kings of the earth and the great ones and the generals and the rich and the powerful, and everyone, slave and free, hid themselves in the caves and among the rocks of the mountains, calling to the mountains and the rocks, 'Fall on us, and hide us from the face of him who is seated on the throne, and from the wrath of the Lamb, for the great day of their wrath has come, and who can stand?'" (Rev. 6:15–17).

Who indeed?

The Grace of God

• • • • • •

But the free gift is not like the trespass.
—Romans 5:15

The whole Bible is about grace. The Old Testament, at one level, is simply an ongoing saga of man's sin in rejecting God followed by God's grace in accepting man; the New Testament is first the story, and then the application, of the biggest grace-moment in history. Whether you read about Abraham or David or Peter or Paul, you find Scripture littered with people who didn't get what they did deserve (otherwise known as mercy), and did get what they didn't deserve (otherwise known as grace). Grace is everywhere.

However, there's something about Paul's treatment of grace in Romans 5 that beats all the others, so we're going to do something unlike most of the rest of this book, and study it in detail. Paul is arguing that, just as we die "in" Adam—we die not because of our individual sins, but because we have our sin credited to us through someone else—so we come to life "in" Christ, getting eternal life not because of our individual acts of righteousness, but because we have our righteousness credited to us through someone else. But Paul can't bring himself to leave it at that. He is so amazed at the grace of God, and particularly the shocking differences between dying in Adam and living in Christ, that he spends three verses describing them.

The sentence we started with seems, at first glance, to be very obvious. Of course the free gift—the grace of God shown in Christ—is not like the trespass: One is positive, and the other negative. But if you look at the next few verses, Paul is saying more than this. He is not just saying that man's sin has negative results and God's grace has positive results, as if the trespass was like losing 1–0 and the gift like winning 1–0. That would be so obvious, it would hardly be worth saying. He is saying that grace and its results *are disproportionate* to sin and its results. He is saying that the trespass is like losing 1–0 and the gift like winning 100–0. The next few sentences give four reasons why.

"For if many died through one man's trespass, much more have the grace of God and the free gift by the grace of that one man Jesus Christ abounded for many" (5:15).

What does "much more" mean here? It cannot be talking about quantity, because all men die for their sin. I don't think it can mean "much more certainly" either, because both death (in Adam) and life (in Christ) are completely certain. I think what Paul is getting at is something like "much more definitively," or "much more lastingly." Think about it: Death in Adam is not the last word. It has been written over people's lives in pencil. It is visible in the lives of unbelievers, but it is always capable of being rubbed out and replaced, as it has been for all of us who have repented. The gift of grace in Christ, on the other hand, absolutely is the last word. It has been written in indelible ink, engraved on the hands of God for all who believe, incapable of removal or substitution or loss. Death in Adam can be overcome by God's grace; God's grace cannot be overcome by anything. Grace is God's great ace, untrumpable, far more significant, permanent, and definitive than the results of the trespass.

"And the free gift is not like the result of that one man's sin. For the judgment following one trespass brought condemnation, but the free gift following many trespasses brought justification" (5:16).

Now, Paul contrasts grace ("the free gift") and judgment ("the result of that one man's sin"), in two ways. First, condemnation is an appropriate response to sin, but a free gift of justification is a thoroughly inappropriate response to it. It's common sense—trespasses should lead to condemnation, and they definitely should not lead to justification. So grace is different from judgment in its appropriateness, if I can put it like that.

Second, condemnation followed "one trespass," but the justification followed "many trespasses." This makes the contrast even more shocking! If one sin leads to condemnation, surely many sins should lead to many condemnations. But they don't, because the gift is of a different scale from the condemnation, and God's grace is of a different magnitude from his judgment. Instead, they lead to justification, through the scandalous, outrageous grace of God.[1]

"For if, because of one man's trespass, death reigned through that one man, much more will those who receive the abundance of grace and the free gift of righteousness reign in life through the one man Jesus Christ" (5:17).

Here, the contrasts we have seen already all apply, but if we look carefully, we see that a further factor has been thrown in. The subject of the first main clause is death: "Death reigned" through one man's sin. We would expect the subject of the second main clause to be life: Death reigned, but now life reigns. That's the contrast, surely? But when we look, we see the subject is not life, but us. The rulers are "those who receive God's abundant provision of grace." We have not simply been transferred from one ruler to another, but transferred from being subjects under a ruler to rulers ourselves, in the new realm of life.

God's grace is definitively lasting, totally inappropriate, unreasonably enormous, and completely transforming. He not only takes away what we do deserve (the wrath of God, separation from him, and death) but also gives us what we do not deserve (justification, union with Christ, and eternal life), not to mention seating us with him in heavenly places in Christ. That's grace: Talk about amazing!

Endnote
1. *A wonderful treatment of the extravagance of grace can be found in Philip Yancey,* What's So Amazing About Grace? *(Grand Rapids, MI: Zondervan, 1997).*

WAIT AND WORSHIP

"Amazing Grace," written by the former slave trader John Newton in 1779, is the most popular hymn in the English language, and has spent more weeks in the music charts than any other song except "My Way." Because everyone knows the tune, there is no excuse for not singing it; I would suggest finding a solitary place, like a field or a hill, and spending some time singing aloud to God for his grace.

> *Amazing grace! How sweet the sound*
> *That saved a wretch like me!*
> *I once was lost, but now am found;*
> *Was blind, but now I see.*
>
> *'Twas grace that taught my heart to fear,*
> *And grace my fears relieved;*
> *How precious did that grace appear*
> *The hour I first believed!*
>
> *Through many dangers, toils, and snares,*
> *I have already come;*
> *'Tis grace hath brought me safe thus far,*
> *And grace will lead me home.*

The Lord has promised good to me,
His Word my hope secures;
He will my Shield and Portion be,
As long as life endures.

Yea, when this flesh and heart shall fail,
And mortal life shall cease,
I shall possess, within the veil,
A life of joy and peace.

The earth shall soon dissolve like snow,
The sun forbear to shine;
But God, who called me here below,
Will be forever mine.

When we've been there ten thousand years,
Bright shining as the sun,
We've no less days to sing God's praise
Than when we'd first begun.

If you like your songs about grace a little bit more upbeat, then the following are superb.

"Your Grace Is Enough" by Chris Tomlin and Matt Maher, © spiritandsong.com (BMI), 2003.

"Grace" by Stuart Townend and Fred Heumann, © 2002 Thankyou Music.

"I'm Alive" by Simon Brading, © 2005 Thankyou Music.

"Jesus, My Only Hope" by Mark Altrogge, © 2002 Sovereign Grace Praise (BMI).

YAHWEH IS MAJESTIC

• • • • • •

O Yahweh, our Lord, how majestic is your name in all the earth!
You have set your glory above the heavens.... When I look at
your heavens, the work of your fingers, the moon and the stars,
which you have set in place, what is man, that you are mind-
ful of him, and the son of man that you care for him?
—Psalm 8:1–4

If you want to understand God's majesty, all you need is a Bible and
a night sky. The Bible will give you the words: majesty, awe, splendor,
wonder. But looking at the stars will give these words something of their
real meaning. Vocabulary often loses its power through exaggeration, as
football players become "awesome," skyscrapers "majestic," and so on. But
the night sky gives a hint of what these words actually mean when they are
used of God. The moon and the stars, set in place by God, loudly trumpet
the utter majesty of Yahweh's name and the utter irrelevance of mine.

Take a journey with me. If you're reading this reflection at a time and place where you can see some stars, get outdoors and take a torch so you can keep reading. If you're not, skip to the next reflection, and come back to this one when it's a clear night. Then step outside, and look up.

By far the closest thing you can see is the moon, if it happens to be in the sky where you are. True, a jumbo jet would still take two weeks to fly to it, but it's much nearer than anything else up there. The moon is pretty amazing, because it doesn't produce any light of its own, and just shines because of the reflected light of the sun; it's basically a big lump of rock. I sometimes wonder whether God put it there simply to show you and me what it means to shine every day in the reflected light of the Son (2 Cor. 3:18). Either way, the moon is a remarkable piece of work.

Now find the brightest star you can see. That is Sirius, or the Dog Star, and it is about two and a half times the size of our sun. Light, which takes 1.3 seconds to get from the moon to the earth, takes eight *years* to get here from Sirius. And this is one of the very closest stars to earth. In galactic terms, it's the family two doors down on the other side of the street. You should be starting to get a sense of what the word "majestic" means.

To get farther out into space, look for Orion's Belt (that's the three stars that form an almost completely straight line). Under the right-hand end of the belt, there is a stunning purple shape that looks like a seahorse, called the Horsehead Nebula, which only telescopes can see. (This is truly baffling to me, because no one except God even knew it was there until 1888. If I had made something even a fraction as beautiful, I would have made sure everyone knew about it.) This nebula is 1,600 light years away—so the light you can see tonight, traveling at 5.88 trillion miles per year, left it when the Roman Empire was coming to an end. To get from one side of it to the other, at the speed of light, would take three and a half years. "Is not God high in the heavens? See the highest stars, how lofty they are!" (Job 22:12).

Now, if you've got a clear night, face southeast, and use your peripheral vision (which is more sensitive to light) to find the Androm-eda Galaxy: an oblong, misty smudge in the sky. If you've found it, you are now looking at the farthest object visible with the naked eye. It is an island of 300 billion stars, over 2.5 million light years away. That is unthinkable. If you're anything like me, these numbers became a bit unreal awhile ago, but hopefully they are making you realize something of how small you are, how majestic Yahweh is, and how ridiculous it is that he even knows who you are.

David, with none of these numbers but with the same night sky in front of him, saw exactly what you see, and wondered aloud why the God who made the heavens would have humankind in his atten-tion. He understood the smallness of man; in Psalm 39 he described the life of man as "fleeting," "a few handbreaths," "nothing," "a mere breath," and "a shadow." He also understood the majesty of Yahweh, having seen the moon and the stars that he set in place. And taking the two together, he could not understand why God would care for him: "When I think of your heavens, the work of your fingers, what is man that you are mindful of him?"

It is important that we have this perspective. Louie Giglio writes: "We are fleeting mortals. Frail flesh. Little specks. Phantoms. If this fact makes you just a tad bit uncomfortable, you're not alone. Invariably, when I talk about the vastness of God and the cosmos, someone will say, 'You're making me feel bad about myself and making me feel really, really small,' as if that's the worst thing that could happen. But the point is not to make you feel small, rather to help you see and embrace the reality that you are small."[1]

You are. So am I. Any prolonged period of staring up into the heavens, like you have just been doing, will tell you that. More than that, though, it will tell you that you serve a God of majesty—not like that of a skyscraper, or even a monarch, but the kind of star-casting, galaxy-forming, space-filling splendor that gives the word "majesty" back its real meaning.

O Yahweh, our Lord, how majestic is your name in all the earth!

Endnote
1. *Louie Giglio,* I Am Not But I Know I AM *(Portland, OR: Multnomah, 2005), 51.*

Yahweh Is Mighty

· · · · · ·

Mightier than the thunders of many waters, mightier than
the waves of the sea, Yahweh on high is mighty!
—*Psalm 93:4*

One of my favorite things in the world is at the end of my road. See if you can guess what it is.

It is very large, and it has shaped the history of the whole world. Most people on earth would have heard of it, but it would stir different emotions for each person. When I was young I was scared of it, but now I appreciate it and love staring at it. If you like reading military history, generations of armies tried to work out how to overcome it, and it was largely responsible for Britain's dominance of the world in the nineteenth century. If you like reading crime, it has never been stolen, damaged, or defaced, even though no one guards it overnight. If you like reading about science, it is made of two remarkable substances:

the world's most common molecule, and the world's most powerful preservative. If you prefer the arts, it has inspired numerous paintings, poems, and pieces of music, not to mention a whole load of sports. And if you're into the Bible, it is used in Psalm 93:3–4 as a comparison, to show how mighty God is. It is the sea.

Like Yahweh, the sea can be the most relaxing, restful, peaceful thing there is. Old friends and young lovers alike come and gaze at it, reflecting on how vast and soothing it is. People pay small fortunes for houses by the sea, or for holidays in the Caribbean. A sunset over the sea is almost indescribably beautiful to those who have never seen it. The steady, gentle, rhythmic whispering of the waves can make almost any problem seem insignificant; somehow, looking at the sea can calm our souls and refresh our spirits. Like Yahweh.

Yet, like Yahweh, the sea can also be the scariest thing in all creation, because we cannot control it. It is wild and frightening, with the power to overturn ships, collapse cliffs, and even wash away entire cities. Waves can reach heights of thirty-five yards or more on the open seas, and the ocean can be fierce, deafeningly noisy, and violently powerful. I have been in a passenger ship in the North Sea during a storm so strong it set oil-rigs off their moorings; even on the top deck of this huge ship, the spray alone was like having a water cannon fired at you from point-blank range. No amount of technological invention has managed even to stem the advance of the tide, far less prevent tropical storms from causing destruction. The sea is uncontrollable by man, and in the centuries-old battle between the sea and man, the sea always wins.

So when the psalmist looks for things to which he can compare Yahweh, he picks the sea. You think the sea makes a racket during a seasonal storm? he asks. You should hear the roar of Almighty God. You were shocked and afraid when you saw the waves during a hurricane or tsunami? Now imagine the one who created those waves, imagine how much power he must have to stir up a cyclone. You think the sea is wild, untamable, powerful, and mighty? You don't know what those words mean until you've seen the untamable, powerful, mighty God. "Mightier than the thunders of many waters, mightier than the waves of the sea, Yahweh on high is mighty!"

Yet it is not just that God is mightier than the sea. He actually made it. The difference between God and the sea is not a difference of degree, like that between a Steinway piano and a Casio keyboard. It is a difference of category, like that between the keyboard and the person who makes pianos and plays concertos on them. The oceans may look uncontrollable—and to us, of course, they are—but Yahweh is totally sovereign over them. As Job, when he made the mistake of questioning God's justice, was asked:

> Or who shut in the seas with doors when it burst out from the womb, when I made clouds its garment and thick darkness its swaddling band, and prescribed limits for it and set bars and doors, and said "Thus far shall you come, and no farther, and here shall your proud waves be stayed?" (Job 38:8–11)

Yahweh is so in control of all things that even the raging seas are operating within limits, bars and doors clearly set by Almighty God. Not one wave can overstep the boundary that Yahweh has established.

The sea can be both powerful and peaceful at the same time, like Yahweh. The sea is there day in, day out, whether we notice it or not, like Yahweh. The sea cannot be domesticated by man, like Yahweh. The sea is frightening and fierce and mighty, like Yahweh. But the sea was created by God, as a pointer toward his astonishing glory and breathtaking power. In a God-shrinking and irreverent generation, we must be careful to remember that he is God Almighty, not God All-matey. Without doubt, Yahweh on high is mighty.

THE HAPPINESS OF GOD

● ● ● ● ● ●

The happy and only Sovereign, the King of Kings and Lord
of Lords, the only one to have immortality, living in light
no one can approach, whom no one has seen or is able to
see, to whom be honor and power forever. Amen.
—1 Timothy 6:15–16 (author's translation)

The Sovereign God is happy. He is happy in a far deeper and more lasting way than any of us can know. He is not contentedly contemplative, like Buddha, or occasionally optimistic, like us, but jubilantly joyful, deeply delighted, and seriously satisfied. The word *makarios*, which I have translated as "happy" but which in your Bible is probably "blessed," is the same word that starts all of the beatitudes in Matthew 5, and which describes those who enter the wedding supper of the Lamb in Revelation 19. In other words, it is talking about a serious, lasting, ecstatic joy.

This often goes unnoticed, but if you read Scripture, it is everywhere. Psalm 104:31 talks about God "rejoicing" in his works. Isaiah 62:4 refers to the "delight" God has in his people, and Zephaniah 3:17 describes Yahweh "rejoicing with gladness" and "exulting with loud singing" over them. The second fruit of the Spirit listed in Galatians 5:22 is "joy." In 1 Timothy 1:11 (NIV), Paul calls the good news "the glorious gospel of the happy (or blessed) God." Then we have the rejoicing Trinity, as God the Father was "well pleased" with his Son at his baptism (Luke 3:22), and Jesus "rejoiced in the Holy Spirit" (Luke 10:21).

There is more. Jesus indicates in Matthew 25:21 that to go into God's presence is to "enter into the joy of your master," an astonishing verse because it shows that being where God is means experiencing pure, undiluted happiness. This, of course, is exactly what the psalmist said: "In your presence is fullness of joy; at your right hand are pleasures forevermore" (Ps. 16:11). And perhaps most definitively of all, there is Psalm 115:3, which says simply, "Our God is in the heavens; he does all that he pleases." Pleasure, happiness, joy, delight, gladness: God experiences them all, and in far greater measure than we do.

The reason for amassing these texts (and there are many more) is to show that the happiness of God is not a new idea designed to fit the desires of a hedonistic society, but a vital part of biblical teaching. In fact, if you follow the Son of God through the Gospels, you will see how extraordinary it is that anyone could see God as anything other than wonderfully happy. His first miracle was to turn water into wine at a wedding. He feasted repeatedly, so much so that he was told off for it by the Pharisees, and described himself as one who "has come eating and drinking." He gratefully received the extravagant pouring of expensive perfume over him on two separate occasions. He told parables about parties and banquets, and the joy of old women and shepherds. As Tim Hansel put it: "The Bible is full of merriment. The feast outruns the fast. It is crammed with spitted kids and lambs and fatted calves, grapes, pomegranates, olives, dates, milk, and honey."[1]

Astonishingly, God was even joyful on the lowest, blackest day there has ever been, when Jesus died on the cross. It was awful, and bleak, and sinful. It was the most intensely painful and hideous thing that anyone has ever experienced. At one level, Father and Son were in utter anguish, separated from one another for the first and only time, and personally experiencing the full effects of sin. Yet at another level, the deep and lasting victory that was being won in the process proved a source of great joy. The process was unspeakably terrible, but the result would bring such glorious consequences that even in the darkest moment in history, there was cause for happiness:

"Yet *it pleased Yahweh to bruise Him*.... He shall see the labor of His soul, and *be satisfied*. By His knowledge My righteous Servant shall justify many" (Isa. 53:10–11 NKJV).

"Jesus, the founder and perfecter of our faith, who *for the joy that was set before him* endured the cross, despising the shame, and is seated at the right hand of the throne of God" (Heb. 12:2).

These verses pose a problem for some people, because they cannot conceive of how God could be angry and heartbroken and happy all at once. Yet we experience simultaneous emotions all the time—I can be elated at scoring a goal, sad that my wife did not see it, disappointed that we did not win the game, and angry about a previous refereeing decision, all at once—so it should not surprise us that God, who is far more complex than we are, can as well. The fact is, in every decision the Lord has made, there is a deep and lasting happiness that outlives all other feelings. Certain of the goodness of his purposes, and permanently delighted by the glories of his cause, his creation, and his character, God is and can be nothing but happy.

This happiness is something God loves sharing with his creatures, and he hates it when they settle for less. As you read through Scripture, notice the number of times it says "Delight yourself in Yahweh," or "Rejoice in the Lord!" We were not intended to be grumpy, or even apathetic, beings. We were made to be joyful, happy creatures, in the image of our joyful, happy God. Remember, the Israelites were ordered to keep five feasts every year; the longest book in the Bible is a book of songs; and there is an entire book about the joy of sex. The happy God created his people to be happy, too.

This is such good news! We will never experience God in a bad mood, overcome by regret or depressed about a bad choice someone has made. He is grieved and he is saddened, but just as Paul was "sorrowful, yet always rejoicing" (2 Cor. 6:10), he remains joyful, blessed, glad, and delighted. In other words, the happy and only Sovereign.

Endnote
1. Tim Hansel, When I Relax I Feel Guilty (Colorado Springs: David C. Cook, 1981), 43.

THE SPEAKING ONE

· · · · · ·

*See that you do not refuse the Speaking One. For if they did not
escape when they refused the one who warned on earth, how much
less shall we escape if we turn away from the one from heaven!*
—Hebrews 12:25 (author's translation)

God speaks. He speaks from the third verse of Genesis to the second-
to-last verse of Revelation. If he didn't, there would be no stars, no
earth, no Israel, and no gospel. But creation dawned with the phrase
"God said"; salvation dawned with the phrase "the Word became";
and speech has been part of his character throughout history, so much
so that Hebrews calls him "the Speaking One." God has always been,
and still is, a speaking God.

God speaks with a voice of creation. Study Genesis 1, and you will
find that the chapter is structured to show that all God had to do was
to speak, and it happened. Creation myths from other cultures in this

period describe gods who competed and fought, argued and jostled, to complete the (for them, extremely difficult) task of making the world. From the first chapter of Scripture, though, Israel's God is set apart from the pagan squabblers, in that he creates by speaking. His word, carrying the full weight of his power, is enough.

Fascinatingly, this did not stop at Genesis 1. God's work of new creation, also, is brought about through speech. Had you noticed that? God's word is the only thing that can bring something out of nothing. In creation, God spoke light out of darkness, and life out of nothingness. In new creation—bringing dead people to life through the Spirit of God—he does exactly the same. Salvation is not simply someone changing their point of view; it is the creation of a completely new type of entity, a born-again person, a corpse made alive through the word of God. It is an entirely supernatural process, brought about entirely by God speaking through the gospel:

"For God, who said, 'Let light shine out of darkness,' has shone in our hearts to give us the light of the knowledge of the glory of God in the face of Jesus Christ" (2 Cor. 4:6).

"Of his own will he brought us forth by the word of truth, that we should be a kind of firstfruits of his creatures" (James 1:18).

"And how are they to believe in him of whom they have never heard? … So faith comes from hearing, and hearing through the word of Christ" (Rom. 10:14, 17).

Light out of darkness, something out of nothing—we exist as new creations in Christ entirely because God speaks. (As Paul makes clear in the last of these passages, this makes preaching the gospel, not just "showing" or "living" it, essential in bringing salvation.)

God also speaks with a voice of sovereignty. In ancient times, a king could speak and it would happen instantly, just because he said it. More recently, when the emancipation proclamation was issued in 1862, slaves were legally free immediately. God's voice is like that, causing things to happen as soon as he speaks:

"The voice of Yahweh is over the waters; the God of glory thunders, Yahweh, over many waters ... The voice of Yahweh shakes the wilderness; Yahweh shakes the wilderness of Kadesh. The voice of Yahweh makes the deer give birth and strips the forests bare, and in his temple all cry, 'Glory!'" (Ps. 29:3, 8–9).

Note the scope of this sovereignty. God's voice brings about every event, from geology (shaking the wilderness) to gestation (making deer give birth). Oh, and it also sustains all things (Heb. 1:3).

Finally, God speaks with a voice of authority. This was the thing the crowds noticed when they heard Jesus teach (Matt. 7:28–29). This does not mean that he was a talented and charismatic speaker, because he is specifically distinguished from "their scribes," and there would certainly have been engaging communicators among this group. What astonishes the people is that he spoke on his own authority, not on someone else's: "You have heard ... but I say ..." When he spoke, things happened. Have a look at the miracles Jesus did, and you will see that not one of them came in response to prayer, and almost all of them resulted from him speaking to the sickness or demon or corpse. Lazarus, come out! Go in peace, your faith has healed you. Be still! His voice alone had the authority necessary to heal.

An interesting example of the authority of the Speaking One has been found through archaeological excavation. In New Testament times,

Tiberias, Korazin, Bethsaida, and Capernaum were four major towns round the Sea of Galilee. Today, Tiberias remains a thriving town, but Korazin has been a ruin since the fourth century, Capernaum was leveled by an earthquake in AD 746 and was never rebuilt, and Bethsaida was so utterly destroyed by successive earthquakes that its ruins were only discovered in 1988. Why were those three in particular so decimated? Because the one who speaks with authority said:

"Woe to you, Korazin! And woe to you Bethsaida! … And you, Capernaum, will you be lifted up to the skies? No, you will go down to the depths" (Matt. 11:21, 23 NIV).

There is something both comforting and sobering about worshipping a God like this. It is comforting, because his voice has an authority and a sovereignty that cannot be challenged, and because he still speaks, bringing salvation and healing and prophetic revelation to his people. It is sobering, because failing to respond to this voice, whether by rejecting the gospel, disobeying Scripture, or despising prophecy, has scary consequences. This is actually the wider context of the passage in Hebrews we started with. The writer, trying to spur on slothful saints, reminds his readers that they are the people of the Speaking One. Previously, God spoke through the prophets, but now he has spoken through a Son (1:1–4). His message was once proved by retribution, but now it is proved by miracles and gifts of the Spirit (2:1–4). Then, his voice shook the earth, but soon it will shake the heavens (12:25–27). So, let us be careful not to refuse the Speaking One.

Instead, let us join those who "in his temple all cry, 'Glory!'"

THE FREEDOM OF GOD

. . . . . .

Moses said, "Please show me your glory." And he said, "I will make
all my goodness pass before you and will proclaim before you my
name, 'Yahweh.' And I will be gracious to whom I will be gra-
cious, and will show mercy on whom I will show mercy. But," he
said, "you cannot see my face, for man shall not see me and live."
—Exodus 33:18–20

Freedom is popular. The final scene of *Braveheart,* the American
national anthem, the French revolutionary slogan, and the rhetoric
of modern war all witness to our passion for it. Yet true freedom is
hard to find. We can limit the constraints on individuals, but this
doesn't make people any more free than the astronaut drifting through
space, free from constraints but totally powerless. We can give people
as many choices as possible, but they always conflict, leading to squab-
bling, crime, and even war. Sinful man, since Eden, has never, in fact,

been free; he has not had the power to do what he wants to do (quit smoking, avoid pornography, forgive his parents), because he has been constrained by sin. Those who are in Christ, as Romans and Galatians triumphantly announce, have been given our free will back, set free in him from the power of sin. Yet even then, as dependent and limited creatures, we are still constrained—by civic laws, physical laws, mother-in-laws, social mores. None of us is independent, so none of us is completely free.

Yahweh is both independent and free, and this comes across very clearly in God's announcement of his name to Moses. In Exodus 3:13–14, Moses asked God for his name, and God told him it was "I am who I am." Here in Exodus 33, it is God's glory that Moses wants to see, but God responds in a similar way, with another two revelations of his name: "I will be gracious to whom I will be gracious, and will show mercy on whom I will show mercy." Together, these three statements show God's sovereign freedom.

You can hopefully see the parallel in form between the three statements: "I _____ who(m) I _____." This sentence structure, even in English, suggests complete freedom. If as a political campaigner I asked you who you were supporting, and you replied that you would vote for who you would vote for, your reply would tell me two things: one, that you were probably free and independent of party politics, and two, to mind my own business! These three names of Yahweh are similar, but on a much larger scale. The first shows God's independence in his being, the last two his independence in his choices. Put another way, the first shows his freedom in whom he is, and the last two his freedom in what he does.

Moses needed to know this. Yahweh had been so angry with Israel for making a golden calf that he had told them he would not go with them, in case he consumed them (33:1–5). Moses was horrified, and cried out for him to relent, so that it would be known Israel had found favor in his sight (33:12–16). When Yahweh agreed, Moses asked to see his glory. Remember: Moses was very aware of how undeserving the people were of God's grace. He had just been commanded to tell them that they were a stiff-necked people. So he was desperately in need of a reason *why*—a reason why God would go with Israel, a reason why he would not destroy them for their sin, a reason why he would continue to drive out their enemies. And, in the revelation of Yahweh's glory and name, he got one.

The reason was simple and shocking: Yahweh was utterly free to choose whomever he wanted. He was not constrained by anything in showing his grace and mercy—not obedience, not consistency, not any quality of his people—but he acted in sovereign freedom. He had not chosen Israel because they were numerous or virtuous, or because Moses was a good leader, but simply because he had chosen them, out of his sovereign grace. Therefore, whether they were a stiff-necked people or not, he would remain gracious to them, simply because he had chosen to be.

This sort of logic moves our goalposts. In Exodus 3, preoccupied with his incompetence and Pharaoh's power, Moses is confronted with God's sovereign being, as if to show that Moses and Pharaoh aren't the basis for God's salvation. In Exodus 33, preoccupied with his people's disobedience and weakness, Moses is confronted with God's sovereign choice, as if to show that the people of Israel aren't the basis for

God's selection. For those of us who live as if we are the center of the universe, this is hard to take. But Yahweh's sovereign freedom is absolute, extending even to the results of rolling dice (Prov. 16:33). His absolutely free choices are not governed by anything outside himself, not even the goodness of his people. If they were, they would not be free choices.

This is how Paul argues in that challenging chapter, Romans 9. He uses this very passage to show that God's glory consists in his free choice, "So then it depends not on human will or exertion, but on God, who has mercy" (9:16). Do you see? If the salvation of Israel, or Isaac or Jacob or you or me, depended on man, then it would not ultimately rest on the free, unconstrained, sovereign choice of God. You were not chosen because of your suitability for salvation, or even your pursuit of God; Yahweh is gracious to whom he will be gracious! Your current obedience or consistency is not the guarantee of God's faithfulness; Yahweh will show mercy to whom he will show mercy! At each stage of Israel's salvation history, and at every point in ours, a sinner's status before God rests on God's free choices, not man's.

Yahweh's freedom means we can (and should!) give him all the credit for our salvation. It also means we can meaningfully pray for unbelievers, since his free choices outweigh theirs. It even means that no one, no matter how evil or resistant to him, is beyond his grace: Idol-worshipping Israelites should prove that. But most of all, it means we can worship a God who is significantly larger than we can imagine, and ask, with Moses, "Show me your glory!"

# STOP AND STUDY

Depending on your background, you may have found the last few pages a bit mind-bending. It could all sound a bit arbitrary, and (if misapplied) could make you feel like human choices were somehow unreal and irrelevant. I had that reaction the first time I encountered some parts of Scripture too, and one of my best friends still maintains that she prefers just to skip over those passages (like Romans 9) that say these things, because she doesn't like them! But I genuinely believe that, if you can get to grips with it, God's sovereign freedom is one of the most powerful, God-exalting, and man-diminishing ideas in the Bible, and it fuels my worship to this day.

Here are a few resources that may help you engage with the (sometimes very difficult) issues involved. These books go into greater depth as you go down the list.

Jerry Bridges, *Is God Really in Control?* (Colorado Springs: NavPress, 2006).
—A practical look at how to think about the sovereignty of God when bad things happen.

John Piper, *The Pleasures of God* (Portland, OR: Multnomah, 2000).

—One of the best books I have ever read, this opens up God's sovereign pleasure and freedom in a way few else ever have done.

R. C. Sproul, *Chosen By God* (Wheaton, IL: Tyndale, 1986).

—A more specific take on the doctrine of election by a leading Reformed scholar.

Wayne Grudem, "Election and Reprobation," in *Systematic Theology* (Grand Rapids, MI: Zondervan, 1994), 669–91.

—The biblical teaching on election from a systematic perspective, in Grudem's typically clear and even-handed style.

Thomas R. Schreiner and Bruce A. Ware (eds.), *Still Sovereign* (Grand Rapids, MI: Baker, 2000).

—A more in-depth presentation of the case for God's sovereign freedom, this book was originally written as a response to Arminianism (if you're not sure what that is, this book will probably be a bit too heavy!).

D. A. Carson, *Divine Sovereignty and Human Responsibility* (Atlanta: John Knox Press, 1981).

—I keep citing Carson, because he is so clear and so biblical—but here he is again, wrestling with one of the most difficult Scriptural tensions.

John Piper, *The Justification of God* (Grand Rapids, MI: Baker, 1983).

—Not for the faint-hearted, this scholarly study of Romans 9:1–23 is outstanding exegesis.

THE FIRE, THE FEAR,
AND THE FRIENDSHIP

• • • • • •

Fire came out from the presence of Yahweh and consumed the
burnt offering and the fat portions on the altar. And when all
the people saw it, they shouted for joy and fell facedown. Aaron's
sons Nadab and Abihu took their censers, put fire in them and
added incense; and they offered unauthorized fire before Yah-
weh, contrary to his command. So fire came out from the presence
of Yahweh and consumed them, and they died before Yahweh.
—Leviticus 9:24–10:2 NIV

Most people struggle with the fear of God. I remember my dad talking to me about it for the first time. After ten years or so of telling me
not to fear, an instruction I usually found very difficult to follow, he
suddenly started saying that there was an exception: that I could fear
God. In fact, that I *should*. It was very confusing, and raised all sorts

of questions. If God is good, why would you fear him? Doesn't that suggest cowering under the table in terror? How can you be in relationship with God and in fear of him at the same time? And so on.

Now, I don't claim to be able to explain this completely, but one thing I discovered has really helped me. I noticed that friendship and fear were two things that characterized man's relationships with all of the most powerful forces on earth, and that the more powerful they were, the more both friendship and fear were appropriate.[1] Early civilizations learned to harness the power of the ox in all sorts of helpful ways, but also knew to run away if it went on the charge. The wind is wonderful, bringing much needed rain, but it can also take your house down. The sea, also, inspires both familiarity and fear, and in fact the people who know it the best, sailors and fishermen, are always the ones with the most respect for it. We all love and delight in the sun, but I presume none of us would like to get too close to it. No one would say that our closeness to any of these things means we shouldn't treat them with respect, or that their power suggests we should avoid them altogether. Friendship and fear go together.

The picture of Yahweh as a consuming fire (Deut. 9:3) is a classic example. Fire is an absolute basic in life; societies cannot get beyond the extremely primitive without it, and it's the first thing the guy on a desert island tries to make. Yet few things can be more dangerous and powerful, as anyone who has ever seen a forest fire, or even a house fire, will testify. Modern man uses fire for more things than any previous generation—cooking, cars, making electricity—yet we fear it more, not less, than we used to. The more developed a culture, the more likely they will be to have fire and emergency procedures, flame-resistant materials, non-spark electricity points, fire breaks in their forests, and the like. The more we learn about fire, the more careful we become about dealing with it.

Israel discovered exactly the same with Yahweh. The more they got to know him, the more they feared him. Moses, with whom Yahweh spoke "face to face, as a man speaks to his friend" (Ex. 33:11), feared him more than anyone else. As with fire, Israel completely depended on him, but grew increasingly aware of how powerful and potentially destructive he was. Like sailors, mountaineers, and firemen, the closer the people got to God, the more fear for him they developed.

There is a superb demonstration of this in the passage we started with. After carefully preparing Aaron's offering, Moses and his brother approach God to see whether it has been accepted, and the glory of Yahweh appears to them: From inside the tent of meeting comes a stream of fire, which instantly burns up the offering in the sight of the people. Overwhelmed by fear (that they serve a God who can send fire at will) mixed with happiness (that such a God has accepted Aaron's offering), the people simultaneously shout for joy and fall facedown. In doing so, they show something crucial: When confronted with a holy God, it is perfectly possible, and in fact necessary, to be delighted and awestruck at the same time. True worship involves both.

Unfortunately, the story does not end there. Fire does not just demonstrate God's favor; it also demonstrates his holiness. Nadab and Abihu, in offering unauthorized fire, treat God without fear, and they are instantly consumed by (surprise, surprise) the fire of Yahweh. Do you see the parallel between the two stories? First, we see a sacrifice offered using the precise specifications God set down, which honors his holiness, and meets with his approval, shown by fire. Then we see the exact opposite: a sacrifice "contrary to his command," which profanes God's holiness, and results in judgment, once again shown by fire. The passage should warn us away from worshipping God according to our preferences, rather than his.

Yahweh is worthy of fear, reverence, and awe, as well as friendship. My guess is, if churches do not find themselves falling facedown as well as shouting for joy on a regular basis, it will not be long before they start offering unauthorized fire. So, as Hebrews says in a passage that echoes this one: "Let us be grateful for receiving a kingdom that cannot be shaken, and thus let us offer to God acceptable worship, with reverence and awe, for our God is a consuming fire" (Heb. 12:28–29).

He certainly is. Let's maintain our friendship, but remember the fire, and keep the fear.

Endnote
1. *The phrase "the friendship and the fear" comes from the album of the same name by Matt Redman (Eastbourne, UK: Kingsway, Survivor, 1997).*

The Glory of Yahweh

· · · · · ·

Such was the appearance of the likeness of the glory of Yahweh. And
when I saw it, I fell on my face, and I heard the voice of one speaking.
—*Ezekiel 1:28*

You cannot fully describe the glory of Yahweh. He is so vast, so multicolored, so glorious in all of his ways, that even man's most thorough
attempts amount to a series of signposts saying, "Look at that." The
most lyrical and dramatic picture of the glory of Yahweh in Scripture,
in my view, is Ezekiel 1, where the images are wonderful: windstorms,
clouds, fire, gleaming metal, lightning, sparkling bronze, lions, oxen,
eagles, wheels, eyes, rushing waters, an expanse of crystal, a sapphire
throne, one with human appearance, rainbows. Yet, after using the
full range of earthly imagery, Ezekiel has hardly scratched the surface.
"Such," he concludes, "was the appearance of the likeness of the glory
of Yahweh." God's glory looked a little bit similar to something that

was ever-so-slightly like this, but words cannot explain how. The glory of Yahweh is indescribable.

So what Ezekiel does, and what the whole Bible does, is to show as many attributes of God as possible, because his glory consists in this: *that he is all of these things at once.* The reason Ezekiel presents us with this bizarre picture of a fiery stormcloud with four-faced living creatures inside, each with their own eye-covered wheel, under a massive crystal wok with a throne on top surrounded by multicolored brightness, is that he is pulling all of Yahweh's apparently irreconcilable characteristics together. He is pointing out as dramatically as possible that Yahweh combines features that, in our minds, simply cannot be held together: lion and ox, windstorm and rainbow, fire and water. This, I think, is what the glory of God actually means.

Our understanding of God is riddled with things we cannot explain properly, and this makes him more glorious, not less. This book has been a mere introduction to some of them: He is one, but Father, Son, and Spirit are all different persons, and all fully God. Jesus is perfectly man and perfectly God, and the living one who died. God has created people who have real choices, yet his sovereign freedom means that his choices are ultimate. The revelation of his name at Sinai showed he was the merciful and gracious God who did not leave the guilty unpunished, a God of simultaneous justice and mercy. Yahweh fills heaven and earth, but has also dwelt in an ark, a tent, a Temple, and now individuals and a people.

No pictures are sufficient to express the full truth about him, not even biblical ones (which is what Ezekiel seems to be conceding in the verse above). In intercession, he is both the one praying and the one being prayed to. In justice, he is the policeman, judge, jury, defense lawyer, and the one who receives the punishment. In the tabernacle, he is both Aaron and the goat, as in an astonishing twist that no one saw coming, the high priest and the sacrifice on the altar turn out to be the same person. In the family, he is father, mother, son, and husband. He is unknowable and known, invisible and revealed, lion and lamb, Prince of Peace and man of war, wrathful and joyful, strength and song, holy and gracious, prophet, priest, and king.

The exuberant and varied use of imagery to describe Yahweh in Scripture is not a sign of confusion or contradiction in the writers. It simply indicates how well they have grasped the depth and riches of God's character, and how beyond our comprehension that character really is. Scoffers will always try to play off Yahweh's attributes against each other, as if the Most High could be reduced to a few simple statements, but we worship a God who is everything Scripture says he is, even if we don't understand how he can be all at once. So don't worry. Children always paint with primary colors, but Van Gogh used thousands. Cheap wines can be described in a word, but top vintages require pages.

The fact is, God is at his most glorious when he is most beyond our understanding. The Trinity, the Word becoming flesh, the cross, the resurrection—these are impossible things to understand, yet they form the center of our faith. This doesn't mean we give up on understanding, or knowing, the living God. The vastness of space is an argument for, not against, purchasing a telescope. But it does mean that as we proclaim the unsearchable riches of Christ, and seek to know the love that surpasses knowledge, we must not be surprised when we encounter truths we cannot grasp and depths we cannot fathom. "The secret things belong to Yahweh our God" (Deut. 29:29).

Remember, the longest sustained vision of God himself that we have in Scripture concluded with Ezekiel acknowledging the massive limitations of his comprehension. One day, we will know more fully. But in the meantime, there is plenty to keep the worship fueled and the glory visible:

> And above the expanse over their heads there was the likeness of a throne, in appearance like sapphire; and seated above the likeness of the throne was a likeness with a human appearance. And upward from what had the appearance of his waist I saw as it were gleaming metal, like the appearance of fire enclosed all around. And downward from what had the appearance of his waist I saw as it were the appearance of fire, and there was brightness around him. Like the appearance of the bow that is in the cloud on the day of rain, so was the appearance of the brightness all around. Such was the appearance of the likeness of the glory of Yahweh. And when I saw it, I fell on my face, and I heard the voice of one speaking. (Ezek. 1:26–28)

INTRODUCTION from the upcoming David C. Cook book

GODSTORIES: EXPLORATIONS IN THE GOSPEL OF GOD

by Andrew Wilson

This book is about the gospel.

Other than that, there's not very much here. If you are looking for practical tips on how to live a successful life, or for academic theology filled with German words you don't understand, then you're looking in the wrong place. All we're going to be doing in this book, from the first page to the last, is exploring the beautiful, triumphant, often heartbreaking—and always glorious—stories that make up the gospel of God. I call them GodStories.

Some readers, I suspect, are already a little bit nervous. The idea of exploring the gospel is fine, but describing it as being made up of lots of pieces—and even worse, lots of *stories*—is bound to put some people off. It all sounds a bit postmodern, as if we no longer have the historic gospel of the last twenty centuries, and have replaced it with a collection of anecdotes and punch lines. It also sounds like you're faced with a sort of pic'n'mix, a Bible buffet, where you can pick your favorite version of the gospel and throw out all the rest. If that's you, then please hear me out until the end of the introduction. All is not as it seems.

On the other hand, there are other readers who (I hope) will be very excited. The people I have in mind are those who find theology to be a rabbit warren of concepts without narratives, a series of points and principles and theories that take all the best bits (like characters and plot twists and heroism) out of the Bible, and leave behind a slightly indigestible result, like eating Wheaties without milk or playing Scrabble without vowels. To such people, the fact that this book is made up of stories—and, far more importantly, the fact that God's Word, and the gospel it describes, are made up largely of stories—should be encouraging. It will certainly increase your enjoyment of theology.

You see, just as we have one God in three persons, and one church made up of many people, so in Scripture we have one gospel made up of many stories. We have one gospel, for sure: a single, unifying, big story (sometimes called a "metanarrative") about God and creation, man and sin, Jesus and rescue. Yet we also have many different ways of telling that big story, because it is too large for us to grasp all at once. Even the pithy summaries in the Bible itself—"your God reigns," and "the kingdom of God is near," and "God raised Jesus from the dead," and "Christ died for our sins," and so on—give different spins on the one big story. So seeing the many GodStories in the one gospel does not reduce that gospel in glory or splendor. Quite the opposite. It dramatically increases it.

This is true of all sorts of big stories, not just the gospel. Say that, instead of writing *The Lord of the Rings*, Tolkien decided to simplify things into a sentence: "Frodo and Sam left the Shire with the ring, faced a number of setbacks, and finally saw it destroyed in Mount Doom and saved Middle Earth." His summary would, in one sense, tell the same story, but it would be dramatically reduced in power and impact, and would probably not have sold millions of copies and been turned into three blockbuster films. *The Lord of the Rings* is about two hobbits and a ring, but it is also about the flight of the elves, the destruction of the forests, the corruption of mankind, the battles for Rohan and Gondor, the return of the king, and the influence the ring has on all of them. So when we read all those other stories, it adds to our understanding of the plot with Frodo and the ring, because it shows us the significance of the main story through its impact on all the others.

With the gospel, this process is far more important, for three reasons. The first and biggest reason is because the glory of God is at stake. If the Bible is stuffed full of GodStories and we only tell one of them, we lose much of the depth and wonder of the gospel, and that diminishes our view of God, just as it would diminish my view of Gordon Ramsay's cooking if I only ate his steamed vegetables.

If, for example, we saw the gospel simply as a story of personal salvation, we would limit its scope enormously, and rob God of the praise that is due to him. Such a view would miss out on the salvation of a corporate people, as opposed to an individual person; it would find very little place for the history of Israel, with which so much of the Bible is concerned; it would marginalize God's faithfulness to his covenant and his multicolored wisdom in the church; and it would ignore the fact that Scripture speaks of the whole of creation, not just human souls, being made new. That doesn't mean that personal salvation doesn't exist, or that it isn't important. But reducing the gospel to personal salvation is like playing Mozart's *Requiem* on the recorder. The melody might be the same, but much of the music's power is lost, and the brilliance of the composer is missed.

There are far more GodStories than there are lines of music in the *Requiem*. God is a far greater composer than Mozart, and he has had thousands of years to craft his composition, with limitless resources and endless imagination. Yet, as with music, God's excellence is shown not just in creating new storylines, but also in fusing them together so that they enhance one another. Mozart brings two melodies together to form a harmony, but Yahweh weaves dozens of GodStories—Abraham, Jacob, Joseph, Moses, David, and the rest—into one another when Jesus arrives on the scene, in ways that make you want to stand amazed and applaud with excitement. Composers frequently write notes that clash with one another to present an unusual sound, but God allows entire plotlines to clash for generations, and then get explained with a twist you would never have predicted (a servant king, for instance). Mozart leaves the final chord in the *Lacrimosa* unresolved for several seconds, but God leaves Psalm 22 and Isaiah 53 unresolved for several centuries before uniting them at the cross with unimaginable power and beauty. So to grasp more of the glory of God, we need to appreciate the range and depth of the gospel, by studying as many of its component stories as possible. More than anything else, the reason for writing a book full of GodStories is to remind us how astonishing and faithful and glorious and worthy of worship is the God who wrote them.

This could not be more important. If God's glory is infinite, and my concept of him is not, then I never stop needing an increased understanding of his greatness. Furthermore, that greatness is many-sided, like a beautiful jewel or a massive mountain; there is nowhere in creation I could stand and see the whole of Mount Everest at once, far less the glory of Yahweh. So I need there to be a whole raft of stories about him that reveal all sorts of aspects of what he has done and how it fits together. Fortunately, by his grace, this is exactly the sort of Bible he has inspired.

Scripture contains something to inspire worship in everyone. To the philosopher, there are GodStories of riddles and revelation, inquiry and truth. To the historian, there are an array of events covering thousands of years and numerous civilizations. To the architect, there are descriptions of temples being established and cities being rebuilt. To the artist, there are GodStories of beauty triumphing over ugliness, order over chaos, new creation over stagnation. For the "chick flick" lover, there is a tale of a complicated relationship with a wonderful man that ends happily ever after; for the action-film fanatic, a story of a hero rescuing the love of his life and saving the world against impossible odds.[1] There are genealogies for the tribesman, parables for the peasant, visions for the mystics and arguments for the intellectuals. And displaying his glory in every one of these GodStories is Yahweh, the I AM, the maker of heaven and earth, and the rescuer of all things. So we need to read all of them, to get as big a view of him as possible.

The second reason for writing, and for reading, a book like this is that people's eternal destinies are at stake. After all, it is the gospel that is "the power of God for salvation to everyone who believes" (Rom. 1:16), and preaching the gospel remains one of the highest callings of every Christian. Without the gospel, people cannot be saved. So it is vital that we know what the gospel actually is, and how to communicate it in ways people understand.

Everyone agrees with that sentence, I'm sure. But read it again, because it is more difficult than it sounds. It is vital that we know what the gospel is, and how to communicate it in ways people understand. Many churches are great at half of this and not so great at the other. Sadly, there are a lot of churches that know the gospel inside out, but put a lot of religious cultural baggage on it, and are therefore not very effective at communicating it to a pluralist and largely pagan culture. On the other hand, there are other churches who have got very good at communicating with the culture, but have in the process lost sight of what they were supposed to be communicating. To be effective missionaries to our culture, we need to be theologically conservative and culturally liberal—strong on what the gospel is, but communicating it without adding religious clutter to it—or, more eloquently, "reaching out without selling out."[2]

Paul is a great model. No one could accuse Paul of not knowing the gospel, or of being scared to preach it. The scars on his back and welts on his face from multiple stonings and floggings would see to that. Yet he used a wide range of GodStories to communicate the gospel, depending on his setting.

To the Jews in Damascus, he proved that Jesus was the Messiah (Acts 9:22). To the Jews in Pisidian Antioch, he preached forgiveness of sins and freedom from the law through Jesus' resurrection (Acts 13:16–41). To the pagans in Lystra, he spoke of the creator God who showed his presence by giving them crops and good weather (Acts 14:14–17). To the pagans in Athens, he proclaimed an independent God who did not need serving, and would one day judge the world (Acts 17:22–31). To King Agrippa and Festus, he shared his personal testimony (Acts 26:1–32). So, although we know from Romans that Paul was utterly convinced of justification by faith, and redemption, and being in Christ, we know from Acts that these weren't always the GodStories he used when preaching to unbelievers. Others, equally true, were often more appropriate to his audience.

Or take a more contemporary example. Many have now heard the story of the Irian Jayan tribe who, on hearing the gospel preached, concluded Judas was the hero and saw no reason to worship Jesus. The missionary, desperately looking for a GodStory they would understand, discovered that this village, after a tribal war, would send a "peace child" to their enemies as a means of reconciliation. So he preached Jesus as God's peace child, and brought salvation to that community. For everyone on earth, no matter how lost, there is a GodStory that will make sense—but we need to know what they are. People's eternal destinies depend on it.

Take the question, for instance: What is the main problem that Eden presents for humanity? Most of us would probably reply that the main problem was guilt, because man sinned and God judged him, and therefore the solution needed was forgiveness. However, this is not necessarily the answer that would be given by much of the world today (or, for that matter, by Abraham or Moses). Many cultures would reply that the primary problem was shame, and therefore that the solution was acceptance, or reconciliation. Others might say it was death, and that what was really needed was an indestructible life. Still others might argue it was about creation being corrupted as a whole, and needing renewal. All of these, of course, are absolutely right answers, and all of them find their fulfilment in Jesus. But preaching a gospel of personal guilt, *even though it is true*, in a context where most people think the main problem to be overcome is shame, or death, or corruption, would limit the effectiveness of the message. A rape victim might not feel she needs to get forgiven (although she still does), but a gospel of freedom, cleanliness, and wholeness might be just the answer she's been looking for.

In none of this are we saying the gospel needs to change. That is the liberal mistake, and it is a terrible one, because it elevates the desires of man above the desires of God, which is idolatry. What we are saying is that there are numerous GodStories in Scripture, and it might be that the best way of saving some of God's image-bearers is to preach a slightly different GodStory than the ones we are used to. The main planks of the gospel—a loving God, fallen humanity, rescue through the death and resurrection of Jesus, and so on—will never alter. The way we nail the planks together might well do.

The third reason for writing *GodStories* is partly a product of the first two, and this is that the health of the church is on the line. At one level, this is obvious: If the church isn't worshipping God properly, or reaching the world with the gospel, then it is a waste of space and time. There is more to it than that, however. Again and again, in the pages of the New Testament, we find writers contending for the gospel because they care about the church.

To the Galatians, the GodStories that Paul wants to reinforce are those about justification by faith, and about Jew and Gentile being one in Christ.[3] The Corinthians, on the other hand, seem to understand that concept, but need a strong reminder about Christ being crucified, their being sanctified, and the bodily resurrection. First John focuses on the incarnation GodStory more than others. Hebrews tells us about the priesthood of Jesus and the superiority of Christ to the major Jewish symbols. In none of these cases is evangelism the point at issue. Instead, a failure to understand various GodStories leads to division and sexual immorality and false teaching and backsliding, respectively. So the health of the church depends on understanding the fullness of the gospel.

We have seen this recently, in the United Kingdom at least, in the debate over the meaning of the cross. Some scholars, observing the contemporary church, noticed that the understanding of the gospel in some circles was fairly narrow, and always revolved around one particular GodStory (called penal substitution). They wanted to remind the church that there were a number of other, very powerful, ways of describing what Christ did for us that had been sidelined, or even forgotten. In doing so, however, some called into question the idea of penal substitution being biblical at all, which is tragic. In response, many churches simply explained why they still believed it was biblical (which it is), but without conceding that it is not necessarily *more* biblical than victory, reconciliation, redemption, and so on (which it isn't). So the health and unity of the church has been compromised, in some cases hugely, because of a failure to understand that there are many God-Stories in Scripture, and they are all true, and they all need to be preached. There is no *pro forma* gospel. God is too big for that.

The good news of God, in fact, needs to be preached to Christians. In all its fullness. The gospel is not just for guest meetings or open airs, as you would think to hear us sometimes, but for the people of God. The outstanding explanation of the gospel in Romans, remember, was written to Christians; Paul tells Timothy to preach the word to his church until he's blue in the face (2 Tim. 4:2); and Paul's aim to visit the capital of the world was generated by a desire to preach the gospel amongst the church there (Rom. 1:15). If preaching the gospel to the church means simply reiterating the call to repent and be saved every week, then it is no wonder that so many preachers (and listeners) struggle. But if it means explaining to the church the full extent and scope of the GodStories in Scripture, then you could preach for a lifetime and never repeat yourself.

Thank God that there's so many to go around. If you're in an introverted community of mature Christians, you can study the mission of God. If you love seeing people saved but you aren't quite sure what to do with them when they are, you can look at freedom from sin. Frustrated artists can look at God's beauty; frustrated activists, his justice. If you don't get the Old Testament, then you can look under every verse and every rock until you find Christ. If you only get the Old Testament, then see how all of God's promises are now yes and amen. Whoever you are, wherever you're reading this—down the beach, on the bus, by the bed, in the bath—you can find a GodStory that will expand your view of God, and revel in it. Then you can experience the joy of sharing it, in a culturally appropriate way, with someone who doesn't know it yet. The world has nothing in comparison.

So we need to know, and preach, and live the gospel. The good news that shines through every GodStory will bring us closer into worship, push us further into mission, and draw us closer into community—face down, flat out, all in. This book is just an introduction to a few of them. But it might change your life, all the same.

GodStories usually do.

Endnotes
1. Adapted from David Murrow, Why Men Hate Going to Church *(Nashville: Nelson, 2005), 15.*
2. This phrase is the subtitle of Mark Driscoll's excellent book on the subject, Radical Reformission *(Grand Rapids, MI: Zondervan, 2004).*
3. If, that is, we recognize that Galatians might tell more than one GodStory at once, rather than (as sometimes happens) playing them off against each other. For an excellent explanation of how we can and should embrace both these GodStories together, see Stephen Westerholm, Perspectives Old and New on Paul: The "Lutheran" Paul and His Critics *(Grand Rapids, MI: Eerdmans, 2004).*

About the Author

Andrew Wilson has degrees in theology from Cambridge University (MA) and London School of Theology (MTh), and a passion to communicate the truth about God.

He has been an assistant brand manager for global giant Procter & Gamble, then a strategy consultant in London for two years, and is now a full-time member of the leadership team at Kings Church, Eastbourne, in the United Kingdom.

Andrew has taught in North America and continental Europe, and at various international conferences, and his books have been translated into several languages. He currently directs and teaches two courses in systematic theology in the United Kingdom.

Andrew is married to his wife, Rachel, and is the author of *Deluded by Dawkins?* (Kingsway) and *GodStories: Explorations in the Gospel of God* (upcoming from David C. Cook).